THE CATHOLIC UNIVERSITY OF AMERICA
CANON LAW STUDIES
No. 255

# THE *SEPTIMAE MANUS* WITNESS

*A Historical Synopsis and a Commentary*

BY
THE REVEREND TIMOTHY J. MCNICHOLAS, J.C.L.
PRIEST OF THE ARCHDIOCESE OF CINCINNATI

A DISSERTATION

SUBMITTED TO THE FACULTY OF THE SCHOOL OF CANON LAW OF THE CATHOLIC UNIVERSITY OF AMERICA IN PARTIAL FULFILLMENT OF THE REQUIREMENTS FOR THE DEGREE OF DOCTOR OF CANON LAW

THE CATHOLIC UNIVERSITY OF AMERICA PRESS
WASHINGTON, D. C.
1949

*Nihil Obstat:*
LUDOVICUS MOTRY, S.T.D., J.C.D.,
*Censor Deputatus*

*Washingtonii, die 11 Julii, 1949*

*Imprimatur:*
JOANNES T. McNICHOLAS, O.P., S.T.M.,
*Archiepiscopus Cincinnatensis*

*Cincinnati, O., die* 12, *Julii,* 1949



MURRAY & HEISTER—WASHINGTON, D. C.
PRINTED IN THE UNITED STATES OF AMERICA

 9

*To*
*His Excellency*
THE MOST REVEREND JOHN T. MCNICHOLAS
*Archbishop of Cincinnati*

# TABLE OF CONTENTS

# FOREWORD

Since the promulgation of the new Code of Canon Law in 1918, the Holy See has found it necessary to issue various Instructions concerning the canonical procedure to be followed in the trying of matrimonial cases. The main object of this work is the Instruction issued by the Sacred Congregation of the Sacraments on May 7, 1923. This Instruction gave special legislation to be followed in cases involving the impediment of impotence and alleged non-consummation of marriage.

It is the purpose of this study to examine and discuss only one section of the above-mentioned Instruction, namely, that section which deals with the *septimae manus* witness. This question will be considered in its relationship to the canonical legislation of the Code. All other forms of evidence submitted in such cases will be mentioned only briefly in discussing the comparative values of the various proofs in their relation to the testimony of the *septimae manus* witnesses.

A brief resumé of the background of the *septimae manus* witness is added with the hope that it will be of some service in aiding the reader to understand the nature of this type of proof. This historical summary is not an exhaustive study; the lack of the full sources and the lack of time have rendered such a study impossible.

The writer wishes to express his sincere gratitude to His Excellency, the Most Reverend John T. McNicholas, Archbishop of Cincinnati, for the opportunity of advanced study in Canon Law; to the members of the faculty of the School of Canon Law for their valuable assistance; and to his fellow students, the priests of the School of Canon Law, for their aid and encouragement in the preparation of this dissertation.

# INTRODUCTION

To look back through the history of the Church and to search out the origin and the source of the Church's laws is not merely a matter of historical interest, but a matter of importance to the canonist as well. The relationship of the canonical laws of the present to past legislation must be considered if one is to grasp the complete meaning of present-day legislation.[1]

The procedural law of the Church as enacted in the Fourth Book of the Code[2] is applied in practice most frequently in marriage cases. In any trial, whether ecclesiastical or civil, evidence holds the place of paramount importance. The question of what evidence and what type of evidence is required for the establishment of the proof is contingent upon the particular case at hand.

In the vast majority of ecclesiastical trials, and especially so in marriage cases, the final decision is based upon the testimony furnished by the witnesses. The rôle of the witness in giving his testimony imposes a serious obligation, especially when the validity of the marriage is under consideration. The types of witnesses, together with the character and the scope of their testimony, as found in the canonical procedure of the Church, are many and various. For the present purpose, in order that the consideration may be limited to a particular type of witness, only two general classifications will be made.

1. There are witnesses who are cited that they may give testimony to the occurrence of some fact, or to the existence of some impediment. These are witnesses in the strict sense of the word.[3]
2. There are witnesses whose testimony is limited to a declara-

---

[1] Cf. canon 6.

[2] Canons 1552–2194.

[3] "Testis est persona a iudice et a partibus distincta, quae ad fidem faciendam de aliquo facto adhibetur." Beste, *Introductio in Codicem,* (Collegeville, Minnesota: St. John's Abbey Press, 1938), p. 799 (hereafter cited *Introductio*).

tion regarding the character of the contesting parties. Their sole purpose in the trial is to testify to the credibility of the statements made by the contestants in a particular trial.[4]

In the present-day legislation of the Church this latter type of witness is specifically adapted to cases in which the marriage is being impugned on the grounds of impotence or non-consummation.[5] Although this type of witness is also used in cases in which the validity of Sacred Ordination is questioned, throughout this work it will be dealt with only in relation to marriage cases. Its use in cases concerning Sacred Ordination will be treated in an Appendix. Although not a witness in the strict sense, the one who gives this type of testimony is called in the technical language of procedure " a *septimae manus* witness." This type of witness has been incorporated into the procedural law of the Church from the ancient Germanic system of law.

To understand the part played by these witnesses one must prescind entirely from the concept of " witness " as it derives from Roman Law. De Smet (1868–1927) tried to see in the *septimae manus* witness some likeness to the witnesses demanded in Roman law for the presenting of a bill of divorce.[6] However, it must be pointed out that the seven witnesses prescribed by the Emperor Augustus in the Lex Julia were demanded, not that they might give testimony or evidence concerning the character of the person seeking the divorce, but that they, at some later date, might be called upon to prove that the divorce had taken place.[7] Their sole purpose, as found in Roman law, was that they might bear witness to the proper fulfillment of the contract.

---

[4] Canon 1975, § 2.

[5] Canon 1975, § 1 and 2.

[6] De Smet, *Betrothment and Marriage,* (2 ed., 2 vols., Herder: St. Louis, 1925), I, 254 (hereafter cited *Marriage*).

[7] Bücher, *The Roman Law Contract,* (London, 1895) pp. 26–27.

# PART I

## HISTORICAL SYNOPSIS

# CHAPTER I

## THE GERMANIC LAW OF PROOF

### Article 1. *General Notions*

For a clearer understanding of the type of witness known as the *septimae manus* witness as found in the present-day law of the Church, one must consider at least in outline form some of the features of the Germanic law. In considering the institutions of the medieval Germanic law, one does not find a system of law as highly developed as that of the Romans. The system of Roman law had practically reached its peak at the time when the tribes from the North migrated into Central Europe. These tribes which settled in the Germanic countries were not the legal-minded people of the Roman provinces. The semi-barbarous customs which had served them so well in their Northern Kingdoms were followed in their new homes.

The formal legal trial as found in Roman law was something unheard of and entirely foreign to their ideas of justice. Juridical action in the early Germanic courts implied a very summary process. Among the earliest forms of proof found in these courts was the oath. The oath was taken not as a means of settling the case, but in order that the justice of the claim made by the accuser, or the counter claim in the defendant's rebuttal, might be substantiated.[1] In the actual proceedings of the trial the court had little power over the eventual outcome. The task set for the court was not that of passing a sentence of acquittal or of conviction, but of laying down and fixing rules by which the parties themselves proved their respective claims.[2]

Among the people from the North there were very strong

[1] Lingard, *The Antiquities of the Anglo-Saxon Church,* (Philadelphia, 1841) p. 185; Moriarity, *Oaths in Ecclesiastical Courts,* The Catholic University of America Canon Law Studies, n. 110 (Washington, D. C.: The Catholic University of America, 1937), pp. 12–14, (hereafter cited *Oaths*).

[2] Moriarity, *Oaths,* p. 13.

family ties. Whenever a quarrel took place between two individuals, it resulted in a quarrel between the families, and the quarrel all too frequently was settled upon the battlefield. It was only in subsequent times that one finds these people taking their quarrels into court.[3] The early Germanic court was a representation of the community, so that what was proved to the court was accepted as proved to the whole community. After the plaintiff had stated his case and had taken an oath upon the justice of his claims, the defendant had in one way or another to prove his innocence. The most common form used in vindication of oneself was to take an oath with a certain number of oath-helpers.

Many look upon this form of oath as the oldest form of proof which is to be found in the Germanic law. This certainly seems to be the case in those periods in which the Germanic nations were fully established in their European Kingdoms. From their early history as a European people it seems rather difficult to substantiate this practice. Nevertheless, many historians look upon the oath as the ordinary means of proof in the *Lex Salica.*[4] Glasson is of the opinion that the oath did not provide the most common method of proof, but merely a means that was resorted to in exceptional cases.[5] He further pointed out that the law itself admitted the use of the oath only in cases in which certainty could not otherwise be had.

Generally the oath of the party himself was not sufficient. If the oath was to have any real value in bringing about his subsequent vindication, it was necessary that others take the same oath with him. These others, oath-helpers as they were called, could be

---

[3] Esmein, *The History of Continental Criminal Procedure,* Vol. V of the Legal History Series (Boston: Little, Brown & Co., 1927) p. 34.

[4] Cf. Dill, *Roman Society in Gaul in the Merovingian Age* (London, Macmillan, 1926) p. 58 (hereafter cited *Roman Society*).

[5] Glasson, *Histoire du Droit et des Institutions de la France* (7 vols., Paris, 1889), III, 474: ". . . si l'on généralement d'accord pour admettre que le preuve par cojureurs est de droit commun dans la plupart des législations germaniques, ce point soulève quelques cependant difficulté en ce qui concerne la loi salique. Beaucoup d'autres pensent que le preuve par cojureurs est aussi un moyen ordinaire d'établir droit dans la loi salique. Nous croyons cependant qu'il était autrement . . ." (hereafter cited *Institutions de la France*).

his parents, friends, relatives, or neighbors. The degree of their suitability was determined by their relationship with the individual. Parents were always given preference, for through them the status of the contesting party as a free man could easily be determined. Friends, relatives, and neighbors, by their testimony and co-operation, showed that he was a man of good repute among his fellow men. These oath-helpers in no way gave any direct testimony regarding the case itself. By their co-operation with the party in the oath, they testified to his sincerity, and swore that his oath concerning this particular affair was certainly trustworthy.

This type of proof, however, was limited in its application; it was not permitted in all cases alike.[6] One's condition in life or one's reputation often stood in the way of the taking of this oath. One who had previously been convicted of perjury could neither take the oath himself nor could he be an oath-helper for another.[7] In the case of those who, for one reason or another, were not permitted to take the oath, another form of proof was used. As a rule this was in the form of a duel or the judgment of God, as it was called, or one of the many forms of the ordeals which were prevalent at that particular time.[8]

### Article 2. *Oaths and the Oath-Helpers*

The earliest form of this type of proof, in which the claims of one of the contesting parties were settled by the oath taken in conjunction with the oath-helpers, is found in the laws promulgated by King Gundobad (473–516) between the years 480–490.[9] Throughout the early Germanic laws these oath-helpers were called "*sacramentales,*" from the word "*sacramentum*" which meant oath; or "*coiuratores,*" from the fact that they took their oath together with the party at trial.[10]

[6] *Lex Alamannorum, Monumenta Germaniae Historica, Leges,* (5 vols., ed. by G. Pertz, G. Waitz, H. Brunner, Hannoverae: 1835–1889) III, p. 56, tit. 40 (hereafter cited *MGH, Leges*).

[7] Brunner, *Deutsche Rechtsgeschichte* (2 ed., 2 vols., by C. von Schwerin, München und leipzig: Verlag von Duncker & Humblat, 1928), II, 528 (hereafter cited *Rechtsgeschichte*).

[8] Glasson, *Institutions de la France,* III, 472.

[9] *Liber Legum Gundebati,* tit. 8, n. 1—*MGH, Leges,* III, 536.

[10] Brunner, *Rechtsgeschichte,* II, 513–515.

In the *Lex Frisonum* the number of the required oath-helpers was determined by the type of crime in question, or by the dignity of the person accused or offended.[11] Seventeen were required in the case of a free man (*liber*) accused of committing a crime against a nobleman. On the other hand, if a nobleman was accused of murdering a free man he needed only seven. In cases of theft, a free man needed six to take the oath with him, in order to be acquitted.[12] It was not, however, essential for the validity that the oath-helpers be of the same class and dignity as the man accused. For a person to prove that he was free of debt, the number of the oath-helpers was always determined in proportion to the amount of money involved.[13]

Originally these oath-helpers were selected by the party himself. Yet it is clear from the *Lex Alamannorum* that this was not always the case, for at times some, indeed, were chosen by the party, while others were chosen by the court.[14] The seriousness of the accusation or of the alleged crime often required that one produce six, twelve, or even as high as seventy-two such oath-helpers.[15]

In his *History of the Franks,* St. Gregory, Bishop of Tours (573–593), pointed out that this system of proof had been adopted and used frequently by the Church.[16] Three Bishops and three hundred men took the oath with Queen Fredegundis to establish the fact that the child brought to the church for baptism was the legitimate son of King Chilperic I (561–584).

Although the oath taken by the oath-helpers was a primary source of proof, it was not the only proof recognized in the Germanic courts. Whenever the liberty of taking this oath was in

---

[11] *Lex Frisonum,* tit. 1—*MGH, Leges,* III, 656.

[12] *Lex Frisonum,* tit. 3—*MGH, Leges,* III, 661.

[13] *Lex Frisonum,* tit. 9—*MGH, Leges,* III, 666.

[14] *Lex Alamannorum,* tit. 30: "Si quis missum ducis infra provinciam occiderit, tripliciter eum solvat sicut lex habet. Si negare voluerit quod non fecisset, sicut lex . . . iuret duodecim nominatos et alios duodecim electos." *MGH, Leges,* III, 54.

[15] *Lex Baiuvariorum,* tit. 13—*MGH, Leges,* III, 315–316; *Lex Ribuaria,* tit. 62—*MGH, Leges,* V, 202–219.

[16] Gregoire de Tours, *Histoire de Francs,* (2 vol., nouvelle edition, Paris: René Poupardin, 1913) II, 317.

any way restricted, other forms of proof were relied on. Slaves, perjurers, prisoners, and magicians were excluded from taking the oath.[17] In cases wherein a person was unable to secure the necessary helpers, or if he did not wish to avail himself of this mode of proof, he was free to prove his innocence by submitting to the ordeal.

### Article 3. *The Ordeal*

During the period of the Merovingian Frankish Kingdom the ordeal served simply as a subsidiary or secondary means of proof. The theory behind the institution called the ordeal was this: God, the all wise and ever watchful guardian of justice, would protect and shield from harm any and every innocent party.[18] The ordeal consisted of certain practices or trials which one underwent in order to prove one's innocence. Concerning its origin there has been a great deal of discussion. Strictly considered, it is not of Germanic origin.[19] Nevertheless, it was within the Germanic Kingdoms that the ordeal was to reach its peak of popularity and perfection of method. Its most frequent form was the duel, which was termed the *iudicium Dei.* In this type the ordeal was found in the Lex Burgundionum,[20] and only a free man was permitted to engage in it. All slaves and women could make use of it only by means of a substitute. The idea behind the duel differed from that which motivated the oaths. In the oath the oath-helper called upon God to witness his testimony, which in the duel God was called upon to judge and to manifest His will by affording protection to the innocent party.[21] A duel was waged as a means of settling a

---

[17] Whalen, *The Value of Testimonial Evidence in Matrimonial Procedure,* The Catholic University of America Canon Law Studies, n. 99 (Washington, D. C.: The Catholic University of America, 1936), p. 20 (hereafter cited *Testimonial Evidence*).

[18] "La preuve par jugement de Dieu à l'epoque franque, est un moyen le plus souvent subsidaire, consistant dans certaines pratiques dont le resultat est l'oeuvre de Dieu, qui fait ainsi connaître la vérité." Glasson, *Institutions de la France,* III, 505.

[19] Cf. Glasson, *Institutions de la France,* III, 505–510.

[20] *Lex Burgundionum,* tit. 7, n. 2—*MGH, Leges,* III, 537.

[21] "Dans le sermont, on se borne à prendre Dieu à témoin, dans les ordalies, Dieu devient luimême le juge et manifeste directement se volonté." Glasson, *Institutions de la France,* III, 506; Moriarity, *Oaths,* p. 15.

war between the Vandals and the Alemani. The champions of each army were chosen to engage in a duel, thus leaving the outcome to the hand of God.[22]

The duel, however, was not the only form of the ordeal known to the Germanic people. Very frequently they resorted to the ordeal of fire,[23] in which the defendant was obliged to carry a red-hot iron over a given distance.[24] The distance was determined by the seriousness of the alleged crime. If during this time his hands were not burnt, he was believed to have established his innocence.[25] This practice became very ritualistic, and it was not an infrequent occurrence to find the individual preparing for it by fasting and penance. This type of ordeal was recounted also by Gregory of Tours.[26]

The ordeal of the ploughshare was very similar to that of the fire. In this the accused was forced to walk bare-foot over red-hot ploughshares. Burnt feet were always a sign of guilt.[27] Another species of this ordeal was that in which scalding hot water was used.[28] After the arms were withdrawn from the water they were wrapped in a bandage for three days. If on the third day when the bandage was removed the arms showed any signs of being burnt, the guilt of the defendant was considered as proved.[29]

The ordeal of cold water [30] consisted in this: the hands and the feet of the accused were tied, and then he was cast into the river. If he floated he was innocent; if, on the other hand, he sank, he was considered as guilty.[31]

The Lex Ribuaria extended to strangers the privilege of the oath in conjunction with the oath-helpers. However, in cases wherein

---

[22] Gregoire de Tours, *Histoire des Francs,* II, 33; *The History of the Franks by Gregory of Tours,* translated by O. M. Dalton (2 vols., Oxford: The Clarendon Press, 1927), II, 209.

[23] *Lex Burgundionum,* tit. 1—*MGH, Leges,* III, 486.

[24] Brunner, *Rechtsgeschichte,* II, 579.

[25] *Lex Ribuaria,* tit. XXX—*MGH, Leges,* V, 222.

[26] Gregoire de Tours, *Histoire des Francs,* II, 32.

[27] *Lex Baiuvariorum,* tit. 1—*MGH, Leges,* III, 468.

[28] Cf. Dill, *Roman Society,* p. 58.

[29] *Lex Frisonum,* tit. 6, 8, 9—*MGH, Leges,* III, 661; *Lex Baiuvariorum,* tit. 1—*MGH, Leges,* III, 486; Cf. Brunner *Rechtsgeschichte,* II, 581.

[30] Moriarity, *Oaths,* p. 15.

[31] Brunner, *Rechtsgeschichte,* II, 551.

the required number of co-swearers could not be found, the stranger was forced to undergo the ordeal of fire.[32] In some instances the stranger was given the choice between the oath, the casting of lots, and the ordeal.[33]

### Article 4. *The Reaction of the Church to the Germanic Method of Proof*

When one considers the attitude of the Germanic mind in regard to legal formalities and the deep-rooted character of the practices engendered thereby, it becomes easier to understand why the continual opposition of the Church had such little effect. It was entirely beyond the scope of the Church's power to uproot many of these pagan practices. In a general way many of them had to be tolerated, at least for a time. The Church was at least partially successful in combating the duel by submitting in its stead the ordeal of the cross.[34]

In this ordeal, after suitable prayers, both parties presented themselves before a cross with arms outstretched in the form of the cross. The one who was the first to allow his arms to drop to his side was defeated, and the truthfulness of the other party's claim was sustained.[35] This type of ordeal came into high favor and was used very frequently in trials among the clergy. With Charlemagne ascending the throne in 768 the Church was to find a strong supporter for its stand. While he firmly believed in the ordeals,[36] he attempted to purify them of many of the pagan practices. He decreed that the oath was to be taken in the church and

---

[32] *Lex Ribuaria,* tit. 31, n. 1—*MGH, Leges,* V, 224.

[33] *Lex Ribuaria,* tit. 5—*MGH, Leges,* V. 200.

[34] *Council of Verberie* (756), caput 17: "Lorsque' une femme prétend que son mari n'a pas eu commerce avec elle, ils seront sousmis l'un et l'autre a l'épreuve de la croix et si telle est vérité, ils seront séparés et la femme poura faire ce qu'elle voudra." Hefele-Leclercq, *Histoire des Conciles* (10 vols. in 19, Paris: Libraire Letouzey et Ané, 1907–1938) III, pars II, 919–920.

[35] Brunner, *Rechtsgeschichte,* II, 559.

[36] ". . . ut omnes iudicium Dei credunt absque dubitatione." *Monumenta Germaniae Historica, Legum Section II, Capitularia Regum Francorum,* (2 vols., ed. A. Boretius, Hannoverae, 1883–1893), I, 150 (hereafter cited *MGH, Capitularia*). Cf. Brunner, *Rechtsgeschichte,* II, 540.

the lots were to be cast upon the altar or upon the relics of the Saints.[37]

For any satisfactory evaluation of the attitude of the Church towards this mode of proof as found in the Germanic laws, one must accept the distinction as drawn by the Decretists and the Decretalists between the *purgatio canonica* and the *purgatio vulgaris*.[38] The ideas underlying these two types of proof are clearly indicated by the terms themselves. By means of the oath or the ordeal to which the party subjected himself, he without any question of doubt purged himself of all guilt. The *purgatio canonica* was understood as that form of purgation which consisted solely of the oath, whether taken by itself or in conjunction with a number of oath-helpers. On the other hand the *purgatio vulgaris* referred to that form of proof which had as its basis the same specific form as the ordeals.

[37] *Lex Frisonum,* tit. 14—*MGH, Leges,* III, 667.

[38] C. 1, X, *de purgatione canonica,* V, 34; Compliatio I, c. 8, *de purgatione canonica,* V, 29; cc. 1, 2, *de purgatione vulgari,* V, 30.

# CHAPTER TWO

## THE INFLUENCE OF GERMANIC LAW ON CANONICAL PROOFS

### Article 1. PURGATIO CANONICA

From the earliest ages that form of proof which consisted mainly in the oath, whether taken by the individual alone or in conjunction with others, had the approval of the Church. The earliest references found in the *Decretum Gratiani* are pseudo-Isidorian texts. The first of these, presented as a letter of Pope Celestine I (251–253), was in fact composed from the text of the Council of Constantinople in the year 448.[1] Pope Gregory the Great (590–604) prescribed the oath as a means of proof for a certain Bishop Leo in the year 592, by which the latter might clear himself of a false accusation,[2] and again for another Bishop in the year 602, when the latter's accuser failed to prove his accusation.[3]

Gregory of Tours spoke of canonical purgation as being used in the Frankish Kingdom as early as the year 582.[4] The letter which Gratian ascribed to Sixtus III (432–440), in which this Pope supposedly spoke of purging himself,[5] was in reality composed from a text of the *Liber Pontificalis*, as Freidberg (1837–1910) pointed out in his annotation to the text of the letter in question.[6] Gregory II (715–731) in a letter to a certain Boni-

[1] Cc. 1, 2, C. II, q. 5; Jaffé, *Regesta Pontificum Romanorum ab condita ecclesia ad annum post Christum natum MCXCVIII* (2 ed. curaverunt G. Wattenbach, S. Loewenfeld, F. Kaltenbrunner, P. Ewald, 2 vols. in 1, Lipsiae, 1885–1888) (hereafter cited as *Jaffé*), n. 115; Hinschius, *Decretales Pseudo-Isidorianae et Capitula Angilramni* (Lipsiae, 1863), p. 172.

[2] C. 6, C. II, q. 5; *Jaffé*, n. 1183.

[3] C. 7, C. II, q. 5; *Jaffé*, n. 1871.

[4] Gregoire de Tours, *Histoire des Francs*, II, 307.

[5] C. 10, C. II, q. 5: ". . . et facto concilio, cum magna examinatione satisfaciens omnibus (licet evadere aliter satis potuissem, suspicionem tamen fugiens), coram omnibus me purgavi, me scilicet a suspicione et emulatione liberans."

[6] Duchesne, *Le Liber Pontificalis* (Paris, 2 vols., 1886–1892) I, 232.

face (726) advised him to take the oath of purgation in public in order to prove himself innocent, if no witness could be found to testify for him.[7] Even while he was Pope (800), Leo III (795–816) took this oath in self-defense,[8] and in a supposed letter to Charlemagne, which was incorporated in the latter's capitular decrees in 803, it is claimed that Leo suggested that it be used by the priests to clear themselves of false accusation.[9]

The Council of Mainz (851) decreed that a priest could clear himself only if seven priests of the same rank would take the oath with him.[10] In the case of a deacon only three other deacons were necessary. Benedict the Levite in his compilation falsely attributed this canon of the Council of Mainz to the Council of Agde (506).[11] The Council of Worms in the year 868 ordered the oath of purgation to be taken by Bishops and priests as a means of removing suspicion,[12] and if a theft occurred in a monastery, the monks were required to clear themselves by first taking this oath, and then assisting at the Mass offered by the Abbot, during which they were required to receive Holy Communion.[13] In the Council of Tribur

---

[7] C. 5, C. II, q. 5: *Jaffé,* n. 2174; Mansi, *Sacrorum Conciliorum Nova et Amplissima Collectio* (53 vols. in 60, Paris, 1901–1927) XII, 245 (hereafter cited Mansi).

[8] C. 18, C. II, q. 5; "Quamobrem ego Leo Pontifex Sanctae Romanae Ecclesiae purifico me in conspectu vestro coram Deo et Angelis suis." This latter has come down to us from a Roman Ordo, and is recorded in *MGH, Leges,* II, 15.

[9] C. 19, C. II, q. 5. This epistle commands Bishops to impose the process of purgation on priests who had been accused of crime. This canon was not from the pen of Leo III as Gratian believed. The evidence that this was the work of Charlemagne himself is conclusive. Cf. Berardi, *Gratiani Canones ab Apocrophis Discreti,* (3 vols. in 4, Venetiis, 1777) Pars II, tom. II, p. 203, (hereafter cited *Gratiani Canones*).

[10] C. 12, C. II, q. 5; *MGH, Leges,* I, 413.

[11] With reference to this Council of Adge, Van Espen, (1648–1728) *Ius Ecclesiasticum Universum Ceteraque Scripta Omnia,* (Venetiis, 5 vols. 1769) III, t. 8, n. 45., pointed out that this decree was not to be found among its acts. Although the right of purgation by oath was very old in the Church, it can not be said with certainty that it was recognized at the time of the Council of Adge.

[12] C. 22, C. II, q. 5: Hefele-Leclerq, *Histoire de Conciles,* IV, Pars I, 463.

[13] C. 22, C. II, q. 5.

in 895 it was prescribed that this oath was to be taken with twelve others as a means of proving one's innocence.[14]

### Article 2. PURGATIO VULGARIS

Although the Church had sanctioned the use of the *purgatio canonica,* it never approved of its counterpart, the *purgatio vulgaris.* It is to be remembered that in the Germanic countries the influence of Christianity was but beginning to be felt. The various ordeals were just as essential to the Germanic legal system as were the strict formalities of proof in Roman law. These practices had been carried on for centuries. In order to begin its mission, the Church could not but tolerate many abuses. The idea of the ordeals was so deep-rooted that even centuries after their conversion the Germanic tribes were very reluctant to give them up.

Early in the sixth century St. Avitus, Archbishop of Vienne (490–519), had tried to suppress all ordeals, but his efforts went for naught. At the beginning the Church tried to minimize the barbarity attached to the ordeals by clothing some of the less pagan practices with prayers and other religious ceremonies. The Ecclesiastical authorities were particularly opposed to the duel, and in many instances they were able to substitute in its place the ordeal of the cross. It was not until the ninth century, however, that a concentrated effort could be made against all ordeals. Even then some high churchmen supported the long standing practice of the ordeals.

In the year 840 Agobard of Lyons (816–840) condemned the duel as opposed to the teachings of Christianity.[15] On the other hand, Hincmar of Rheims (845–882) in the year 860 gave his approval to its use.[16] In the year 855 the Council of Valence forbade the duel, and decreed that anyone who died as the result of a duel could not be given Christian burial.[17] Kerin [18] pointed out

---

[14] Hefele-Leclerq, *Histoire des Conciles,* IV, Pars II, 701.

[15] *Liber adversus Legem Gundobaldi; Liber contra Iudicium Dei,*—Migne, *Patrologiae Cursus Completus, Series Latina* (221 vols., Parisiis, 1844–1864) CIV, 125, 254 (hereafter cited *MPL*) ; *MGH, Leges,* I, 515.

[16] *Epistola ad Hildegardum—MPL,* CXX, 161.

[17] Hefele-Leclerq, *Histoire des Conciles,* IV, pars I, 207.

[18] *The Privation of Christian Burial,* The Catholic University of America

that this council considered death by this means to be the equivalent of suicide.

During the earlier years of the struggle against the use of the ordeals, the Church had remained silent. But in the year 867 Pope Nicholas I (858–867) refused to allow it as a means of settling the marriage dispute between King Lothair (855–869) and his wife, Queen Theutberga.[19] Pope Stephan VI (885–891) in 885 forbade the ordeals of hot iron and the hot and cold water.[20]

The final legislation by the Council of Trent (1545–1563), which imposed the penalty of excommunication, the stigma of infamy, and the confiscation of property on those who took part in the duel,[21] was prepared for by the statutes of Innocent II (1130–1143) in 1130 against all combats,[22] by the law of Pope Celestine III (1191–1198) against duels within the papal territories,[23] and by the decree of the IV General Council of the Lateran (1215).[24]

---

Canon Law Studies, n. 136 (Washington, D. C.: The Catholic University of America Press, 1941), p. 47.

[19] *Epistola ad Carolum Calvum—MPL,* CXIX, 1142–1144; Mansi, XV, 321–322.

[20] C. 20, C. II, q. 5; *Jaffé,* n. 3443; *MPL,* CXXIX, 797.

[21] Conc. Trident., sess. XXV, *de ref.,* c. 19; Schroeder, *Canons and Decrees of the Council of Trent* (St. Louis: Herder, 1941) pp. 251, 561.

[22] *Council of Claremont,* c. IV—"Detestabiles autem illas nundinas vel ferias in quibus milites ex condicto convenire solent. . . . Quod si quis eorum ibidem mortuus fuerit . . . ecclesiastica tamen careat sepultura." Mansi, XXI, 439.

[23] C. 1, X, *de purgatione vulgari,* V, 35.

[24] C. 18—Mansi, XXII, 1006–1007.

# CHAPTER III

## GERMANIC INFLUENCE ON MATRIMONIAL PROCEDURE

In determining the possible and the actual influence of the Germanic law upon the Canon Law of the Church, one must bear in mind the position in which the Church and its Bishops found themselves. When the Western Empire gave way before the inroads and the incursions of the Germanic tribes, the Church alone survived the invasion. The old Roman imperial system of government collapsed. In its stead the Germanic rulers established a new system of government, in which the Bishop was to be one of the central figures.

In view of the strong authority and prestige given him upon the collapse of the social order, and in consequence of the respect paid to him by the newly converted Merovingian Kings, the Bishop rose to a position of exceptional influence. It must, however, be pointed out that even under such favorable circumstances the controlling power of the Bishop was limited to disciplinary matters. The Kings retained for themselves all legislative power.[1] This explains the presence, in the early Germanic code, of civil laws concerning the ministers of the Church.[2]

Particularly it is to be noted that all legislation on marriage cases was under the sole domination of the secular authority. Yet, despite this fact, one must not suppose that these secular norms were to any overwhelming extent contrary to the laws of the Church. Most frequently it happened that the laws which had first been promulgated by the Church formed the basis or the

[1] Joyce, *Christian Marriage* (New York: Sheed and Ward, 1933) p. 217.

[2] *Lex Baivariorum,* tit. 3: "Si autem de ministerio ecclesiae aliquid furaverit, id est calicem aut patenam vel palam, aut qualecumque re de infra ecclesia furaverit et probatus fuerit. . . . Et si negare voluerit, secundum qualitatem pecuniae iuret cum duodecim sacramentales in ipso altare."—*MGH, Leges,* III, 271.

foundation for this secular legislation.[3] The Frankish Kings assumed to themselves all power in the judicial as well as in the legislative authority over marriage cases. All cases of nullity were considered as within the sole competence of the court of the King, and the process there employed was entirely a civil affair.[4] Hincmar of Rheims maintained that matrimonial cases could not be tried by the Bishop unless the case had been previously settled by a confession or by a civil judgment.[5]

The strong basis which linked the Church with the State was perhaps greatly responsible for much of the Capitulary legislation which was enacted at that time. Although in a large measure this type of legislation was not opposed to the discipline of the Church on matrimony, the Church as a whole never fully accepted it. Even though the legislation added a sanction, both civil and penal, for many of the laws of the Church, basically it was a usurpation of the legislative power of the Church over its members.

Divorce among the Germanic nations had always been a very simple process.[6] Marriage vows were never considered as binding very strictly. The first step to curb this evil was taken at the Council of Soissons in 744.[7] At the Council of Verberie in the year 756, which was more in the nature of a Royal Capitulary than of an Ecclesiastical Council, there was drawn up a list of causes in view of which divorce was permitted, and the right to remarry

---

[3] ". . . cette législation a pour d'adopter des regles ecclésiastiques en leur conferent la sanction civile ou pénale." Esmein, *Le Mariage en Droit Canonique* (deuxieme edition mise a jour par R. Genestal et J. Dauvillier, 2 toms., Paris: Recueil Sirey, 1929–1935), I, p. 10 (hereafter cited *Le Mariage*).

[4] *Lex Baiuvariorum*, tit. 7: "Si quis contra haec fecerit a loci judicibus separentur et omnes facultates ammitant quas fiscus acquirit."—*MGH, Leges*, III, 297; *Esmein, Le Mariage*, I, p. 11.

[5] *De Divortio Lotharii et Theutbergae—MPL*, CXXV, 653.

[6] The mutual consent of the parties was considered as sufficient to dissolve the marriage. Cf. Esmein, *Le Mariage*, II, 70.

[7] "Similiter constituimus ut nullus laicus homo Deo sacratam feminam ad mulierem habeat, nec suam parentem: nec marito vivente suam mulierem alius accipiat, nec mulier vivente suo viro aliam accipiat: quia maritus mulierem suam non libet dimittere excepta causa fornicationis deprehensa." Hefele-Leclercq, *Histoire de Conciles*, III, pars II, 858.

was accorded to the innocent party.[8] From the earliest days of its history the Church had fought against the evil of divorce. When Charlemagne ascended the throne in 768, the Church was at last to have a champion for its cause. In 789 he convoked an Ecclesiastical Capitulary in which he upheld the Church's stand on the indissolubility of marriage.[9]

The change which brought about the placing of marriage cases solely within the competence of the Church was a slow and gradual one. This change was effected by the growing power of the Bishops and not by any formal grant on the part of the secular princes. The Church's exclusive exercise of jurisdiction over marriage began as a matter of custom, and only much later was it recognized as a matter of right.[10] To assign a definite date at which the Church began to exercise this full jurisdiction seems impossible. The appearance of the pseudo-Isidorian Decretals and the subsequent compilation of Benedict the Levite (847–850) contributed greatly to the increased manifestation of the Church's exercise of jurisdiction in marriage cases.[11]

While quite generally the authors are very indefinite concerning the exact time when the Church supplanted the State in the hearing of marriage cases, all agree that a full recognition was accorded to the Church's jurisdiction in the matter during the tenth century.[12] The full recognition which was given to the ecclesiastical courts comprised not only the things which by their very nature were spiritual, but extended also to every controversy which had any bearing, even in the slightest degree, on the Church or religion.

[8] *Concilium Verberiense—MGH, Capitularia,* I, 40–41; Hefele-Leclercq, *Histoire des Conciles,* III, pars II, 918.

[9] "Item in eadem ut nec uxor a viro dismissa alium accipiat virum, vivento viro, nec vir aliam accipiat uxorem, vivente uxore priore."—*MGH, Capitularia,* I, 61.

[10] Joyce, *Christian Marriage,* 224.

[11] Esmein, *A History of Continental Civil Procedure,* p. 111.

[12] Joyce, *Christian Marriage,* p. 224; Esmein, *A History of Continental Civil Procedure,* p. 25.

# CHAPTER IV

## THE *SEPTIMAE MANUS* WITNESS BEFORE THE COUNCIL OF TRENT

### Article 1. *The Pre-Gratian Period*

The history of the dissolution of marriage on the grounds of impotence on the part of one of the spouses has been subject to many changes. The early Germanic peoples gave very little thought to this problem because their system of divorce was very simple. Divorce by the mutual consent of the parties was always possible.[1] It was only later, after the Council of Soissons in the year 744 had determined the Church's doctrine on the indissolubility of marriage,[2] that any real consideration was given to this question.

Definite legislation for the dissolution of marriages in which one of the parties was impotent was enacted at the Council of Verberie (756), which prescribed that the ordeal of the cross was to be used to ascertain the truth.[3] The Council of Compiegne (757) stated the principle that if disagreement was found in the assertions of the spouses, the word of the husband was preferable and was to be accepted as reliable.[4]

In his *Statuta Salisburgensia* Charlemagne again called for this judgment of the cross before either party was permitted to enter another marriage.[5] However, this form of proof was soon to be rejected by a subsequent Capitulary.[6]

---

[1] Cf. Esmein, *Le Mariage*, I, 261.

[2] Hefele-Leclercq, *Histoire des Conciles*, III, Pars II, 858.

[3] " Lorsqu'une femme pretend que son mari n'a pas eu commerce avec elle, ils seront sousmis l'un et l'autre a l'épreuve de la croix et si telle est vérité, ils seront separés et la femme faire ce qu'ell voudra."—*Councile de Verberie*, c. 17—Hefele-Leclercq, *Histoire des Conciles*, III, Pars II, 918; cf. *MGH, Capitularia*, I, p. 41.

[4] *Concilium Compendiense*, c. 20—*MGH, Capitularia*, I, p. 39; *Lex Baiuvariorum, tit.* 46—*MGH, Leges*, III, 474.

[5] *Statuta Salisburgensia*, c. 15—*MGH, Capitularia*, I, p. 80.

[6] *Capitularia Ecclesiastica* (818–819), c. 27: " Sancitum est, ut nullus dein-

Hincmar of Rheims in a passage in which he spoke of a separation on the ground of impotence stated that the marriage could not be annulled without the judgment of an examination.[7] However, he failed to point out what form of proof was to be relied upon in this instance.

As far as can be ascertained, the use of the *septimae manus* witnesses in the investigating of these cases is a later development. The early history of their use up to the time of Gratian is not traceable with any appreciable degree of clarity. In the *Decretum Gratiani* mention is made of this type of witness on one occasion only, and that in relation to a case of impotence. The document cited by Gratian is a supposed letter of Gregory the Great (590–604) to John, Bishop of Ravenna (578–595).[8]

In commenting upon this cited letter of Gregory, Berardi (1719–1768) stated that this particular letter was unquestionably a forgery. He claimed that the wording of this letter had its source in the Frankish Capitulary of King Dagobert in the year 650.[9]

This letter was attributed to Gregory the Great by Burchard, Bishop of Worms (1002–1025).[10] The collection made by Burchard was to form the basis for the work of many of the subsequent compilers, and it is easy to understand why Gratian was to consider this particular letter as a genuine document. Whether or not this particular letter attributed to Gregory the Great be genuine, its value cannot be overlooked, inasmuch as it does testify that this type of witness and its use was known during the early part of the eleventh century.

Concerning the use of the term *septimae manus,* Feije (1820–1894),[11] Gasparri (1852–1934)[12] and Avanzini[13] held that the

1885), p. 410, n. 1, (hereafter cited *De Impedimentis*).

---

ceps quamlibet examinationem crucis facere praesumat; ne quae Christi passione glorificata est, cuiuslibet temeritate contemptui habeatur."—*MGH; Capitularia,* I, 279.

[7] "Non autem legitimum ut femina, libello synodali porrecto conventui, a sua debeat conjuge separari, aut sine publico examinationis judicio a conjugali valeat jugo disjungi." *De Divortio Lotharii et Theutbergae—MPL,* CXXV, 644.

[8] C. 2, C. XXXIII, q. 1; *Jaffé,* n. 1934.

[9] Berardi, *Gratiani Canones,* Pars II, tom. II, p. 203.

[10] *De Matrimonio—MPL,* CXL, 821.

[11] *De Impedimentis et Dispensationibus Matrimonialibus* (3 ed., Lovanii,

word *manus* (hand) was used to denote the aid given to the parties and to insure them against any suspicion of collusion. On the other hand, Van Espen (1646–1728) [14] and Wanenmacher [15] contended that the word *manus* was used as a symbol to express the credence and the belief that was given to the testimony of the parties. These latter writers regard the use of the *septimae manus* witnesses merely as a means of establishing the credibility of the testifying parties. Considered in this light, the *septimae manus* witnesses were simply the equivalent of the oath-helpers in the Germanic system of law.

With relation to this type of witness, the word *septimae* as referred to *manus* points to the fact that seven such witnesses were chosen. Freisen (1853–1932) stated that no reason could be given as to why seven were originally chosen. He said that the compilers merely accepted the number as given by Burchard.[16] Brunner (1840–1915) traced it back to an old Germanic belief regarding the number twelve. The number twelve was always regarded as a universal number, and hence in the *Lex Saxonum* twelve oath-helpers were always considered capable of producing full proof.[17] Thus when among some tribes twelve oath-helpers supported the attestations of the parties, each party was said to have sworn the half oath, calling *septima* or *sexta manus*, and then full proof was had in the case.[18]

According to the citation given by Gratian,[19] a marriage im-

---

[12] *Tractatus Canonicus de Matrimonio* (ed. nova ad mentem Codicis I. C, 2 vols., Romae: Typis Polyglottis Vaticanis, 1932), II, 295 (hereafter cited *De Matrimonio*).

[13] Cf. *Acta Apostolicae Sedis, Commentarium Officiale,* (Romae, 1909–1929, Civitate Vaticana, 1929—) VI (1914), 515 (hereafter cited *AAS*).

[14] *Ius Ecclesiasticum Universum,* Lib. III, tit. 8, n. 47.

[15] *Canonical Evidence in Marriage Cases* (Philadephia: The Dolphin Press, 1935), p. 116 (hereafter cited *Canonical Evidence*).

[16] Friesen, *Geshichte des canonischen Eherechts bis zum Verfall der Glossenlitteratur* (2 Ausgabe, Paderborn, 1893), p. 342 (hereafter cited *Geshichte*).

[17] Brunner, *Rechtsgeschichte,* II, 520.

[18] "Den halben Eid (*septima* oder *sexta manu*) schworen manche Stämme mit sechs, andere mit fünf Helfern." Brunner, *Rechtsgeschichte,* II, 521.

[19] C. 2, C. XXXIII, q. 1: "Quod si mulier causatur, et dicit: Volo mater esse et filios procreare, uterque eorum septimae manu propinquorum tactis

pugned on the grounds of impotence could be dissolved by the oath of the parties, if their oaths were substantiated by the oaths of seven relatives of each party.

The *Glossa Ordinaria* looked to the *septimae manus* witnesses as affording merely a subsidiary proof or a secundary means of evidence. Rufinus (c. 1190) pointed out that the principals took the oath to the *fact* of the non-consummation, while the relatives swore to their *belief* in the non-consummation of the marriage.[20] Although the witnesses went by the name *septimae manus* it was not always necessary that seven be supplied. At times even two or three such witnesses were held to be sufficient.[21] Since these witnesses testified solely to the character of the parties and did not offer any direct testimony in the case, they did not become involved with the parties if the latter were later convicted of perjury. The *septimae manus* witnesses swore, not to the truth of the statements, but to their belief that the parties were telling the truth.

### Article 2. *The Post-Gratian Period*

Subsequent to the *Decretum Gratiani,* Popes Celestine III (1191–1198) and Honorius III (1216–1227) followed the broad outlines for the impotence trial as given by the document cited by Gratian. Pope Celestine directed that as a last resort proof of the non-consummation of a marriage could be offered by means of oaths. Both the husband and the wife, after having given their oaths that they had been unable to consummate their marriage, had to furnish seven relatives or neighbors who took an oath to the credibility of the parties. Before any marriage could be regarded as dissolved on this score, there had to be a *iustum iudicium* of the non-consummation of that union. If it was then

---

sacrosanctis reliquiis iureiurando dicat, ut numquam per commixtionem carnis coniuncti una caro effecti fuisset, tunc videtur secundas posse contrahere nuptias."

20 Rufinus, *Summa* (Edited by Von Schulte, Giessen: Verlag von Emil Roth, 1892), p. 434.

21 Freisen, *Geshichte,* p. 342. Freisen stated that the Glossators showed their misunderstanding of the idea behind this type of witness when they frequently spoke of two or three such witnesses as being sufficient.

proved that one of the parties was impotent, the other was at liberty to contract another marriage.[22]

The Glossator considered the *iustum iudicium* prescribed by Pope Celestine as a decision which was reached by means of the oaths of the parties, and corroborated by the seven relatives or neighbors. If both of the parties admitted the non-consummation, the three year period in which they were to attempt consummation of their marriage was not necessary, for in this case the additional oaths of the seven witnesses sufficed. For such testimony parents and relatives were always to be preferred. However, in their absence, friends or neighbors could offer this oath if they enjoyed a good reputation throughout the community.[23]

Pope Honorius III (1216–1227) commanded that in a given case the parties who had lived together for eight years and had been unable to consummate their marriage were to be given a declaration of nullity if each with seven witnesses took an oath to affirm the impotence of the man.[24] To the required testimony of the *septimae manus* witnesses he added the requisite sworn testimony of midwives concerning the virginity of the woman.

Considering this citation, the Glossator pointed out that the oaths were sufficient in this case inasmuch as both parties agreed in their testimony. But the oaths were always necessary, for in cases which involved possible danger and spiritual harm for souls every precaution had to be taken. The three-year period during which they were to attempt to consummate their marriage was not to be insisted upon in view of the longer period of time in which the parties already had lived together. The physical examination could be omitted provided that the assertions of the parties were corroborated by the oaths of the *septimae manus* witnesses.[25]

---

[22] C. 5, X, *de frigidis et maleficiatis et impotentia coeundi,* IV, 15; Mansi, XXII, 638; *Jaffé,* n. 14125.

[23] Hostiensis, *In Quinque Libros Decretalium Commentaria* (5 vols. in 3, Venetiis, 1581) Lib. IV, tit. 15, n. 5.

[24] C. 7, X, *de frigidis et maleficiatis et impotentia coeundi,* IV, 15; Potthast, *Regesta Pontificum Romanorum inde ab anno post Christum natum MCXCVIII ad annum MCCCIV,* (2 vols., Berolini: 1874–1875), n. 7832 (hereafter cited Potthast).

[25] Hostiensis, *Summa Aurea* (Venetiis, 1570), p. 355.

# CHAPTER V

# THE *SEPTIMAE MANUS* WITNESS FROM THE COUNCIL OF TRENT TO THE CODE OF CANON LAW

## Article 1. *Canonical Jurisprudence*

The development of the doctrine concerning the use of the *septimae manus* witness in marriage cases during the post-Tridentine period is almost entirely independent of any new legislation on the part of the Church. The last formal act of legislation was contained in the Decretals of Gregory IX (1234), as an act of Pope Honorius III,[1] and it was not until the Instruction "*Cum moneat Glossa*" of the Sacred Congregation of the Council (22 August, 1840) that any new legislation was directly to affect the role of the *septimae manus* witness.[2] Notwithstanding this lack of positive legislation during this period, great progress was made in the application of the principles pertinent to marriage cases submitted to the diocesan tribunals.

While the Fathers at the Council of Trent passed considerable legislation concerning the sacrament of Matrimony with reference to the diriment and the prohibitive impediments,[3] no practical norms or directives were forthcoming from it in procedural matters. From the time of the above-mentioned letter of Pope Honorius III until the middle of the last century, all development concerning the use of the *septimae manus* witness was to come from the interpretations given by the leading commentators of the seventeenth and eighteenth centuries.

---

[1] C. 7, X, *de frigidis et maleficiatis et impotentia coeundi,* IV, 15; Potthast, n. 7832.

[2] *Codicis Iuris Canonici Fontes,* cura Eñi Petri Card. Gasparri editi, 9 vols., Romae (postea Civitate Vaticana) : Typis Polyglottis Vaticanis, 1923–1939. (Vols. VII–IX, ed. cura et studio Eñi. Iustiani Card. Serédi) n. 4069 (hereafter cited *Fontes*).

[3] Sess XXIV, *de ref.,* cc. 2, 3, 4, 5, 6: Cf. Schroeder, *Canons and Decrees of the Council of Trent,* pp. 185–187.

The very nature of the testimony of the witnesses of this kind precluded their use in a vast majority of cases. From the beginning their use had been restricted to cases involving the impediment of impotence relative to marriages which had not been consummated. All cases dealing with impotence and with non-consummated marriages could be grouped under three distinct classifications, depending upon the kind of proof needed in substantiation of the claims of the spouses. These categories were:

1. cases in which there were present physical and evident signs of non-consummation;
2. cases in which there indeed were some indications, but these indications were by no means certain; and
3. cases which were of an entirely doubtful nature.[4]

When the evidence clearly showed that the marriage had not been consummated it could be dissolved immediately.[5]

Pirhing (1606–1679) considered the role of the *septimae manus* witnesses of the utmost importance, so much so that he considered their oath essential in every case for the validity of the sentence.[6] Although he held it was very necessary to employ the *septimae manus* witnesses in the vast majority of cases, Barbosa (1589–1649) recognized cases in which the judge was allowed to dispense with the *septimae manus* witnesses. This oath of the relatives and the neighbors, as he called it, was not absolutely required in those cases wherein the high reputation which the parties enjoyed before the community was already proved.[7] In all other cases it was

---

[4] Sanchez, *Disputationum de Sancto Matrimonii Sacramento Libri Tres* (Antverpiae: 1626), Lib. 7, Disp. 107, n. 2 (hereafter cited *De Matrimonio*).

[5] Reiffenstuel, *Ius Canonicum Universum* (5 vols. in 7, Pariis, 1864–1882) Lib. IV, tit. 15, n. 42.

[6] ". . . requiritur tamen juramentum septimae manus propinquorum . . . Papa (Celestinus) formam dissolvendi matrimonium, ratione impotentiae assignat tamquam praerequisitum juramentum, at cum sit forma probationis jure praescripta, propter eius omissionem vitiatur sententia . . ." Pirhing, *Jus Canonicum in Quinque Libros Decretalium Distributum Nova Methodo Explicatum* (ed. novissima, 5 vols. in 4, Dilingae: 1722), Lib. IV, tit. 15, n. 33 (hereafter cited *Jus Canonicum*).

[7] Barbosa, *Collectanea doctorum, tam veterum quam recentiorum, in ius*

absolutely necessary for the validity of the sentence, unless the physical signs of virginity were absolutely certain.

This added source of proof by the oaths to the credibility of the parties was a guarantee and an insurance against the perpetration of fraud or of deceit in the physical examination conducted by the experts. When the impotence could be proved by self-evident and certain signs, the oath of the *septimae manus* witnesses was not only unnecessary,[8] but even superfluous.[9] Nevertheless, this oath of credibility was always regarded as an important element in removing all possible suspicion from the case.[10] Whenever the impediment was of such a nature that only moral certitude of its presence could be had,[11] the oaths of the parties taken in conjunction with the oath of the *septimae manus* witnesses carried sufficient weight to be considered as a primary source of proof.[12] Inasmuch as a lesser proof was needed in cases where probability was present than in cases which were still altogether doubtful, the oath of the relatives was sufficient to produce that degree of moral certitude which was required before the judge could pronounce a sentence of nullity.[13]

Pirhing went even further. He allowed the judge's sentence to be based upon this oath if there was even the slightest likelihood of the presence of the impediment.[14] In all those circumstances in which there was present nothing more than an indication of the presence of the impediment of impotence or of the fact of the non-consummation of the marriage, the presence of the *septimae manus* witnesses was necessary. Their presence and their oaths in substantiation of the confessions of the spouses were capable of producing the degree of moral certitude necessary for the declara-

---

*pontificium universum* (6 vols. in 5, Lugduni, 1716), Lib. IV, tit. 16, n. 6 (hereafter cited *Ius Pontificium Universum*).

[8] Engel, *Collegium Universi Juris Canonici* (4 vols. in 1, Venetiis, 1760) Lib. IV, tit. 15, n. 19.

[9] Reiffenstuel, *Ius Canonicum Universum*, Lib. IV, tit. 15, n. 42.

[10] Sanchez, *De Matrimonio*, Lib. 7, Disp. 107, n. 3.

[11] Reiffenstuel, *Ius Canonicum Universum*, Lib. IV, tit. 15, n. 42.

[12] Barbosa, *Ius Pontificium Universum*, Lib. IV, tit. 15, n. 6.

[13] Schmalzgrueber, *Ius Ecclesiasticum Universum* (5 vols. in 12, Romae: 1843–1845), Lib. IV, tit. 15, n. 79.

[14] Pirhing, *Ius Canonicum*, Lib. IV, tit. 15, n. 15.

tion of nullity or of the dissolution of the marriage bond respectively. Considered in and of itself, the oath of the *septimae manus* witnesses was never sufficient proof, if, when taken in conjunction with other indications, it did not produce certitude. In cases, then, in which there were present only doubtful signs, a more concrete proof was always demanded. In such cases the judge could never dispense with this added oath which the *septimae manus* witnesses were able to furnish.

Originally a great effort had to be made in every case to secure these witnesses. Seven relatives were asked to take this oath. This specific number and the relationship of these witnesses were factors which were subject to change. In very many cases it was impossible to find as many as seven relatives. In fact, at times no relatives at all could be found. When such was the case, it was within the power of the judge to allow neighbors or friends to be substituted, provided that their reputations were of the highest order.[15] In extreme cases of necessity, in order that undue hardship might not be imposed upon the parties, the judge had the authority to accept a lesser number, but only after it had been proved to him that the required number could not be found.[16]

In those cases in which there was concordant testimony received from the two parties inasmuch as both confessed the presence of the impediment and their inability to consummate the marriage, each party was required to present seven witnesses.[17] Thus fourteen relatives as witnesses were necessary in this particular case. On the other hand, when there was a discrepancy in the testimony of the two parties, and a conflict existed between their statements in such a manner that the one alleged the impediment while the other denied it, then the burden of the proof was always on the one who claimed the non-consummation of the union. In such cases he alone needed the substantiation of the *septimae manus* witnesses for his oath.[18]

---

[15] Reiffenstuel, *Ius Canonicum Universum,* Lib. IV, tit. 15, n. 47.

[16] Sanchez, *De Matrimonio,* Lib. 7 Disp. 108, n. 12.

[17] Pirhing, *Ius Canonicum,* Lib. IV, tit. 15, n. 17.

[18] "Illud etiam notandum, quod, si una parte negante, alter pars conjugum affirmet impotentiam perpetuam, et res probari etiam debeat cum juramento credulitatis propinquorum, non requirantur quatuordecim, seu ex qualibet parte septem, sed sufficiant septem ex parte affirmantis." Reiffenstuel, *Ius*

Concerning the circumstances surrounding the taking of the oath, some canonists were more rigid than others. Although a long-standing custom sanctioned the taking of the oath upon the cross, the usually prescribed form was the one that called for the touching of the Gospels.[19] Because of the fact that the ancient canons were explicit in demanding that the witnesses take the oath by touching the Gospels, Sanchez (1550–1610) held that this circumstance was required for the validity of the oath, so that, if an oath were pronounced merely in the presence of the Gospels without the witnesses' actual physical contact with them, or upon a book which contained only selections from the Gospels, then there arose the necessity of repeating the oath in its proper form. It was only in cases of physical impossibility that a person was allowed to establish physical contact with the Gospels otherwise than by a physical touching of them with the hand. If a person had been deprived of the use of his hands, he could touch the Gospels with his arms or even with his foot.[20]

The distinction between the type of oath taken by the parties and that taken by the *septimae manus* witnesses was clearly pointed out by all the canonists. The parties themselves testified that there was no fraud or deceit underlying their claims, while the *septimae manus* witnesses with their oath testified that they believed the statements of the parties to be true and reliable.[21] If at some later date the oaths pronounced by the spouses proved to be false, the parties themselves were considered guilty of perjury, since they had testified regarding their assured knowledge. But this same guilt was in no way shared by the relatives, since they had furnished their oaths simply regarding the trustworthiness of the parties themselves.[22]

---

*Canonicum Universum,* Lib. IV, tit. 15, n. 51; cf. Sanchez, *De Matrimonio,* Lib. 7, Disp. 109, n. 13.

[19] Schmalzgrueber, *Ius Ecclesiasticum Universum,* Lib. IV, tit. 15, n. 89.

[20] Sanchez, *De Matrimonio,* Lib. IV, Disp. 108, n. 14.

[21] "Consangueni debent jurare quod verisimiliter existiment conjuges verum dicere." Pirhing, *Jus Canonicum,* Lib. IV, tit. 15, n. 17; cf. Reiffenstuel, *Ius Canonicum Universum,* Lib. IV, tit. 15, n. 47; Schmalzgrueber, *Ius Ecclesiasticum Universum,* Lib. IV, tit. 15, n. 89.

[22] Engel, *Collegium Universum Juris Canonici,* Lib. IV, tit. 15, n. 12: "Advertendum quod conjugum juramentum sit *de veritate,* testium vero

### Article 2. PRAXIS CURIAE ROMANAE

The interpretations given by the early canonists were to form the basis for the norms used by the Sacred Congregations in dealing with practical cases. In very many of the cases submitted to the Sacred Congregation of the Council for a possible solution, the signs of the impediment of impotence or of the non-consummation of the union were by no means certain, but rather of a doubtful nature. In the majority of the cases the Congregation refused to accept the oaths of the *septimae manus* witnesses with relation to the determining element.

In itself their oath was considered as incapable of producing the required certitude for the dissolution of the marriage bond.[23] But in all those cases in which the physical examination of the woman showed some positive sign of the non-consummation of the marriage, the Sacred Congregation accepted the oath of the *septimae manus* witnesses as a guarantee that no fraud or deceit had been present in the physical examination.[24] If the parties were subsequently to enter a religious institute in order to pronounce solemn vows, then their oaths were of themselves sufficient. There was no need for them to call upon the *septimae manus* witnesses to substantiate their claims relative to the alleged impediment and the non-consummation of their marriage.[25]

In a case in which the husband denied the allegations of the wife and claimed that the marriage had been consummated, the Sacred Congregation based its decision upon the previous physical examination of the woman along with the oaths of the *septimae manus* witnesses, when it declared the marriage to be null and

---

credulitate, et id ipsum juramentum *de credulitate* . . . imponi solet." Cf. Pirhing, *Jus Canonicum,* Lib. IV, tit. 15, n. 33; Sanchez, *De Matrimonio,* Lib. 7, Disp. 108, n. 15.

[23] S. C. C., *Ianuen.,* 20 maii 1719—*Fontes,* n. 3190—*Thesaurus Resolutionum S. C. Concilii* (167 vols., Romae, 1718–1908), I, 198–200 (hereafter cited *Thesaurus*); S. C. C., *Pragen.,* 27 febr. 1734—*Thesaurus,* VI, 249–251; S. C. C. *Romana,* 19 aug. 1786—*Thesaurus,* LV, 173, S. C. C. *Forolivien.,* 20 sept. 1817—*Thesaurus,* LXXVII, 275.

[24] S. C. C. *Ianuen.,* 16 aug. 1783—Thesaurus, LII, 166.

[25] S. C. C., *Neopolitana,* 11 apr. 1761: ". . . quia ingressus in religionem respicit perfectiorem statum, in cuius assumptione suspiciari nequit de fraudibus et collusone." *Fontes,* n. 3190—*Thesaurus,* XXX, 55.

void because of the impediment of impotence on the part of the man.[26] Taken alone, and devoid of all other proofs, the oath of the *septimae manus* witnesses was never capable of affording ample proof in completely doubtful cases.

When there were no fairly certain signs of the impediment and when the physical examination of the woman furnished no definite indication in the case, the oath of the *septimae manus* witnesses was accepted as adminicular proof only upon the lapse of a period of three years from the original oath of the parties. In order that further proof might be established, the Sacred Congregation demanded that for a period of three years the parties give themselves the opportunity to seek to effect the consummation of their marriage. If after this added period they still testified under oath that their marriage was unconsummated and this oath was corroborated by that of the *septimae manus* witnesses, then the Sacred Congregation was ready to render a favorable decision.[27]

Canonists unanimously considered that in law a marriage was presumed to be consummated. Hence, the oath of the parties together with that of the *septimae manus* witnesses was considered as insufficient proof of the non-consummation, since it could not furnish a direct proof but only a corroborative proof. To dislodge the presumption of consummation a more direct proof was needed.[28] The decisive efficacy of the testimony of the *septimae manus* witnesses was limited to those cases in which the evidence offered by the physical examination or by other proof constituted more than a purely doubtful case.

### Article 3. *The Legislation of the Sacred Congregations*

The development in the use of the *septimae manus* witnesses reflected its most progressive period during the latter half of the past century. The many Instructions issued by the Sacred Congregations set very definite norms to be followed in the method of proving the presence of the impediment of impotence and in

[26] S. C. C. *Asten.*, 2 mar. 1776—*Thesaurus,* XLV, 31–35.

[27] S. C. C., *Pragen.*, 27 febr. 1734—*Thesaurus,* VI, 250; S. C. C., *Ianuen.*, 20 maii 1719—*Thesaurus,* I, 199; S. C. C., *Romana,* 19 aug. 1786—*Thesaurus,* LV, 174.

[28] S. C. C. *Ianuen.*, 16 aug. 1783—*Thesaurus,* LII, 165.

establishing the fact of the non-consummation of the marriage. The preliminary steps were taken in Pope Benedict XIV's Constitution *Dei miseratione* (3 November, 1741).[29]

This Constitution laid the foundation for the special modern procedure which was to be followed in the handling of marriage cases. Whenever there existed a doubt concerning the validity of a certain marriage in view of a possible diriment impediment, the case had to be submitted to a formal trial. As long as the arguments against the validity of the marriage which had been contracted were not evident and obvious, they had to be submitted in a judicial process before the judge could arrive at a moral certitude regarding the validity or the invalidity of the impugned marriage. The intervention of the defender of the bond was essential whenever these cases were submitted to the diocesan tribunal.

While the Benedictine Constitution enacted very definite norms to be followed, it did not make full provision for all possible cases. It contained no mention whatsoever of the *septimae manus* witness in cases of impotence and non-consummation. The Sacred Congregation of the Council, feeling the need and the urgency of some special legislation on this particular point, issued a special Instruction to augment the Benedictine Constitution. This Instruction gave full direction, which all the diocesan tribunals were to follow not only in cases dealing with the impediment of impotence, but also in all cases of non-consummation.[30]

The wording of the Instruction of the Sacred Congregation expressed the absolute necessity of the presence of the *septimae manus* witnesses. On all previous occasions they had appeared merely in the role of a character witness, and accordingly had taken the oath *de credulitate*. Thenceforth they were to be asked to testify not only concerning the character of the principals, but also concerning their testimony. Besides the usual questions concerning the character, the honesty and the trustworthiness of the parties, the defender of the bond was permitted, and even requested, to interrogate the *septimae manus* witnesses with questions concerning the actual marriage. " Had the parties for any period of time, lived together? As far as they knew, had the marriage

---

[29] Benedictus XIV, const. "*Dei miseratione*," 3 nov. 1741—*Fontes*, n. 318.

[30] S. C. C., instr. *Cum moneat Glossa*, 22 aug. 1840—*Fontes*, n. 4069.

been consummated? Had the parties made any attempt to consummate it? If the marriage was never consummated, was this due to the presence of some impediment which made its consummation impossible, or was it due to a separation of some sort which might have resulted from a quarrel?"

This Instruction, then, indicated norms which were complementary to the law of the Benedictine Constitution. The norms to be followed in all cases of procedure were thus definitely drawn up. Success attended their practical application in all places or dioceses where duly constituted tribunals complied with these norms. But in consequence of the inefficiency of some tribunals, or as a result of the lack of trained personnel in the courts which had been organized, these most accurate norms could not be duly followed in every detail. To rectify this situation the Holy Office issued an additional Instruction, which provided a more summary process to be followed whenever the circumstances justified its use.[31]

Regarding the cases of non-consummation, the legislation, in general, remained basically the same. The new Instruction contained only slight changes for these particular cases. Parents were always to be called in as *septimae manus* witnesses, for it was presumed that they were better qualified to testify on these intimate matters than anyone else. If because of some physical or moral impossibility they could not be cited, then an annotation to that effect had to be recorded in the acts of the case. To the list of questions required by the Instruction of 1840[32] slight additions were made. "What was their personal judgment, and that of the people of the community, of the alleged non-consummation of the marriage? Were the parties held in such high regard by the community that their word concerning these matters could substantially be accepted?"[33]

The conditions prevalent in the Orient and also here in the United States frequently precluded an exact adherence to all the

---

[31] S. C. C. Off., instr. *Iudex ad hoc deputatus,* a. 1858—*Fontes,* n. 946.

[32] S. C. C., instr. *Cum moneat Glossa,* 22 aug. 1840—*Fontes,* n. 4069.

[33] ". . . quaenam sit fama tam apud se, quam apud alios de hac praetensa non consummatione."—S. C. C., instr. *Iudex ad hoc delegatus,* a. 1858—*Fontes,* n. 946.

indicated norms. To care for these particular situations, the Holy Office and the Congregation for the Propagation of the Faith each issued a further Instruction. The Instruction from the Sacred Congregation for the Propagation of the Faith to the Bishops of the United States [34] was almost completely copied *verbatim* from the Instruction of the Holy Office for the Orient.[35] These Instructions were so similar, in fact, that in the Instruction which was directed to them the Bishops of the United States were told to consult the Instruction of the Holy Office for all cases involving impotence.

In the section which referred to the *septimae manus* witnesses, the Holy Office directed that, if the best qualified witnesses were in a distant land, the Ordinary of the place in which they were residing was to be asked to procure their testimony. In regard to the actual questions which were to be asked, a few changes were introduced. If the testimony of the *septimae manus* witnesses regarding the non-consummation of the marriage in view of some impediment on the part of either party was in agreement, then the witnesses were to be asked: 1) if the parties had consulted doctors or other experts on these matters; 2) what was the result when this course had been followed; 3) what was their personal opinion and that of the people of the locality concerning the statements and the testimony of the parties.[36]

### Article 4. *The Application of the Instructions*

In consequence of the great stress which had been placed upon the rôle of the *septimae manus* witnesses in the various Instructions of the Sacred Congregations, and also in the wording of the

---

[34] S. C. de Prop. Fide, instr. *Causae matrimoniales,* a. 1883—*Fontes,* n. 4901.

[35] S. C. S. Off., instr. (ad Ep. Rituum Orient.), a. 1883—*Fontes,* n. 1076.

[36] "Interrogandi autem erunt testes praesertim: an cognoscant conjuges, de quibus est sermo; an sciant, utrum libenter mutuoque affectu sese copulaverint, condormierint, matrimoniun consummaverint; quibus et quid experti fuerint; utrum et cuius generis conquestus inter eas exorti, et quaenam eorum causa; unde sciverint quae deponunt: et si ab extraneis ea compererint, quomodo vocentur, et ubinam comarentur. Interrogandi quoque de fama tam apud ipsos quam apud alios circa assertam non consummationem et impotentiam." S. C. S. Off., instr. (ad Ep. Rituum Orient.), a. 1883—*Fontes,* n. 1076.

texts themselves, many doubts were to arise concerning the importance of the testimony of these witnesses.[37] The first Instruction, which had been issued in 1840, was not unmistakably clear in its wording. It had called for the *septimae manus* witnesses, but it did not in any way expressly delimit their testimony as essential exclusively in the case of impotency.[38]

As a result of these doubts and the subsequent confusion, these witnesses were cited in cases which were being tried for nullity on other grounds. In cases presented to the Sacred Congregation of the Council, it appeared that they had been used with a view to establishing proof for a declaration of nullity based on the grounds of "*vis et metus,*" [39] and on the fact of previous illicit intercourse as giving rise to the impediment of affinity.[40] It was his desire for a settlement of this doubtful usage that prompted the Archbishop of Warsaw to seek an interpretation from the Sacred Congregation. He asked if it was necessary to cite the *septimae manus* witnesses in all cases of nullity, or only in those which involved the impediment of impotence or the question of non-consummation. In its reply the Sacred Congregation expressly limited the use of the *septimae manus* to those two mentioned cases.[41]

In keeping with the direction given in the Instructions, the parents were always the first chosen. The order of relationship

[37] Bassibey, *Le Mariage devant les Tribunaux Ecclésiastiques* (Paris: 1889), p. 271: "Jusq'a ces dernières années il etait difficile d'avoir une opinion bien précise sur ce point." (hereafter cited *Le Mariage*).

[38] S. C. C., instr. *Cum moneat Glossa,* 22 aug. 1840: ". . . eiusmodi testimonium septimae manus universim quidem requiri . . ."—*Fontes,* n. 4069; cf. Feije, *De Impedimentis,* p. 439.

[39] S. C. C., *Calven. et Theanen.,* 26 junii 1869—*Fontes,* n. 4214—*Thesaurus,* CXXVIII, 343; S. C. C., *Gnesnen. et Posanien.,* 9 sept. 1894—*Thesaurus,* CLIII, 1302.

[40] S. C. C., *Baionen.,* 12 sept. 1891—*Thesaurus,* CL, 718; S. C. C., *Versavien.,* 25 febr. 1895—*Thesaurus,* CLIV, 151.

[41] S. C. S. Off., 16 jun. 1894—: "1. Sitne in causis nullitatis matrimonii ex quocumque titulo coram Iudice spirituali agitatis necesse exigere, ut testes septimae manus producantur, an vero in solis causis ex capite impotentiae devolutis observandam, in ceteris omnibus praetermitti posse?" Resolutio Sacra Congr. Concilii, re disceptate sub die 16 Junii 1894 censuit respondere—ad 1. Negative a primam partem: et testimonium septimae manus, stricto sensu sumptum, exigi ad corroborandam confessionem coniugum quoad inconsummationem matrimonii." *ASS,* XXVII (1894–1895), 152–153.

was observed whenever possible. By reason of the close ties of relationship the members of the immediate family were better qualified to offer testimony concerning these marriage problems.[42] The early Instructions had called for the testimony and the oath of relatives or friends; yet most frequently better testimony could be obtained from servants who resided in the same house with the parties, or from neighbors who were in close social contact with them.[43] Parish priests and also religious who were closely acquainted with the family were, by reason of their close ties of friendship, in an excellent position to give valuable testimony.[44] In a case presented to the tribunal at Paris three priests appeared in the role of *septimae manus* witnesses.[45]

In the history of the procedure in the Sacred Congregations the canonical norms reflected repeated vicissitudes. The older norms regulating the manner for obtaining canonical proof were, in the course of time, forced to give way to newer ones. The oath of the *septimae manus* witnesses passed from its capacity for furnishing strong proof in itself to a stage where it was but a mere formality, but then again emerged in a new rôle, that of a confirmatory proof. For over a period of more than a hundred years the Sacred Congregation regarded the unsuccessful outcome of the three year experiment on the side of the parties in the marriage as the only real and unfailing means for establishing proof of the invalidity of their marriage on the ground of impotence.

When the consummation of the marriage had from other sources of possible knowledge remained a doubtful issue, the oaths of the *septimae manus* witnesses were accepted only after the lapse of the three-year period.[46] This three-year period of experiment as a possible means for establishing proof of impotence remained in use up until the last century. However, it gradually fell into

---

[42] Bassibey, *Le Mariage*, p. 268, n. 353.

[43] S. C. C., *Molinen.*, 29 mar. 1890—*Thesaurus*, CXLIX, 257; S. C. C., *Mechlinien.*, 10 maii 1890—*Thesaurus*, CXLIX, 363.

[44] S. C. C., *Lavallen.*, 14 iul. 1894—*Thesaurus*, CLIII, 819; S. C. C., *Leopolien.*, 13 iun. 1896—*Thesaurus*, CLV, 416.

[45] S. C. C., *Parisien.*, 17 febr. 1906—*Thesaurus*, CLXV, 253.

[46] S. C. C., *Ianuen.*, 9 sept. 1719—*Thesaurus*, I, 237; S. C. C., *Pragen.*, 27 febr. 1734—*Thesaurus*, VI, 249-251; S. C. C., *Forolivien.*, 20 sept. 1817—*Thesaurus*, LXXVII, 275.

desuetude, and the Sacred Congregation of the Council did not demand it after 1817.[47] Since that time no mention of it can be found in any of the Instructions which have come from the Sacred Congregation within the past century.[48]

Since the beginning of the present century the oath of the *septimae manus* witnesses has acquired greater importance and weight than it had in the immediately preceding centuries. In 1906 a woman who claimed that she and her husband were unable to consummate their marriage was given a declaration of nullity after the testimony of the *septimae manus* witnesses, even though she had refused to submit to a physical examination as a means of acquiring proof of her virginity.[49]

After a woman had already entered into another union she was given a declaration of nullity when her oath along with that of the partner of her first union, namely, that they had never consummated their marriage, was supported by the oath of the *septimae manus* witnesses.[50]

In another case the *septimae manus* witnesses testified not only to the credence that was to be given to the testimony of the parties but also to the fact of the non-consummation when a woman had refused to submit herself to the corporal inspection.[51]

The majority of the late pre-Code canonists considered the testimony of the *septimae manus* witnesses as fully acceptable in most of the cases in which their testimony was admitted in court. Undoubtedly the best and the strongest proof which could be offered was the corporal inspection of the wife. Yet this was not looked upon as absolutely necessary in every case.[52]

If for some reason or other the examination of the woman could not be carried out, or if, although carried out, it served to

---

[47] S. C. C., *Forolivien.*, 20 sept. 1817—*Thesaurus*, LXXVII, 275.

[48] Cf. Cappello, *Tractatus Canonico-moralis de Sacramentis, vol. III, De Matrimonio* (4. ed., Taurinorum Augustae, Romae: 1939), p. 469, n. 373.

[49] S. C. C., *Mechlinien.*, 17 febr. 1906—*Thesaurus*, CLXV, 281.

[50] S. C. C., *Camerocen.*, 11 ian. 1908—*Thesaurus*, CLXVII, 1–2.

[51] S. C. C., *Regien.*, 1 febr. 1908—*Thesaurus*, CLXVII, 34–35.

[52] "Certe ad probanda non secutam consummationem optima probatio est exploratio corporis mulieris. . . . Tamen haec probatio, quamvis potissima, non est absolute necessaria." Lega, *Praelectiones de Iudiciis Ecclesiasticis* (4 vols., Romae, 1896–1901) IV, p. 494, n. 668. (hereafter cited *De Iudiciis*).

prove nothing in view of a previously existing marriage or of illicit relations outside of lawful marriage, then moral certitude of the non-consummation of this particular marriage could be obtained from some other conjectures when they were substantiated by the oaths of the parties and that of the *septimae manus* witnesses.[53] Thus the judge could acquire sufficient moral certitude to call for a favorable decision in the matter.[54]

When the presence of the impediment of impotence had been fully established through a physical examination, then not only the oath of the *septimae manus* witnesses but even the oath of the parties themselves was unnecessary.[55] However, as long as the examination did not serve to furnish proof, either of the presence of the impediment or of the non-consummation of the union, then the oath of the parties with the oath of the *septimae manus* witnesses became a primary source of proof. Still, as a general rule, a more substantial proof was demanded.[56]

In general, the Sacred Congregations always attributed considerable value to the depositions of the parties in their assertions of the impediment or of the non-consummation. Just shortly before the present Code of Canon Law came into effect the Roman Rota gave a favorable decision to a couple who had lived together for sixteen years and whose only proof that their marriage had not been consummated was their oaths supported and corroborated by the oaths and the testimony of the *septimae manus* witnesses.[57] Nevertheless, the Church has always safeguarded the law of the indissolubility of marriage, and hence in non-consummation cases

---

[53] De Becker, *De Sponsalibus et Matrimonio* (2. ed., 2 vols., Lovanni, 1903) II, 419; S. C. C., *Parisien.*, 15 dec. 1894—*Thesaurus*, CLIII, 1149; *ASS*, XXVII (1894), 670 seq.; S. C. C., *Lepolien.*, 13 iul. 1896—*Thesaurus*, CLV, 409—*ASS*, XXIX (1896), 134 seq.

[54] Bouix, *Tractatus de Judiciis Ecclesiasticis*, (3. ed., 2 vols. Paris, 1883) p. 450–451.

[55] Wernz, *Ius Decretalium* (6 vols. Romae et Trati, 1898–1905) IV, 513; S. C. C., *Ianuen., et Viennen.*, 15 dec. 1877—*ASS*, XI (1877) 134 seq.

[56] "Conjugum confessio contra matrimonii valorem probandi non statim habet, imo ipsa confessio conjugum sola per se vi probatoria caret." Meehan *Compendium Juris Canonici* (Roffae, 1899), p. 273. (hereafter cited *Compendium*).

[57] Cf. Wanenmacher, *Canonical Evidence*, p. 374.

the mere confession of the parties was never considered as relieving them of the burden of offering more conclusive proof.

From the concordant testimony of the *septimae manus* witnesses there arises a presumption in favor of the truthfulness of the confession made by the parties. This presumption could serve to strengthen the oath of the parties to such an extent that the judge became fully justified in relying upon it.[58] When the physical examination afforded at least a solid probability to the existence of the impediment, then the decision of the judge could be based upon the oath of the *septimae manus* witnesses.[59] Lega (1860–1935) considered the testimony of the *septimae manus* witnesses as a representative of the whole community to the truthfulness of the spouses in their assertions of the oath or in their confessions before the court.[60]

---

58 Sanguinetti, *Iuris Ecclesiastici Privati Institutiones* (Romae, 1884), p. 452.

59 Smith, *Elements of Ecclesiastical Law* (3. ed., 3 vols., New York, 1888) II, 407

60 Cf. Lega, *De Iudiciis,* IV, p. 493, n. 468.

# PART II

## CANONICAL COMMENTARY

# CHAPTER VI

## THE *SEPTIMAE MANUS* WITNESSES

### Article 1. *The Nature of the* SEPTIMAE MANUS *Witness*

The language of the Code of Canon Law expresses very succinctly the rôle played by the *septimae manus* witnesses in the matrimonial procedure of the Church when it states:

> Testimonium septimae manus est argumentum credibilitatis quod robur addit depositionibus coniugum. . . .[1]

While speaking of the proofs which are to be offered in all cases involving impotence and non-consummation, canonists point out the special types of proof which are to be used in these cases, namely, the testimony of the *septimae manus* witnesses and the corporal inspection.[2]

Canonists are accustomed to make a clear-cut distinction in drawing a line of demarcation between the physical and the moral proof. The physical proof, i.e., the physical examination as conducted by experts, offers a more cogent form of evidence. However, due to circumstances which are beyond the power of the court, it is not always possible to introduce this type of proof. In such cases the moral proof, which is had when the *septimae manus* witnesses by an oath of credibility support the claims of the principal parties, must be relied upon for the evidence.[3]

---

[1] Canon 1975, § 2.

[2] Chelodi, *Ius Matrimoniale iuxta Codicem Iuris Canonici* (3 ed., Tridenti: Libr. Edit. Tridentum, 1921), p. 193 (hereafter cited *Ius Matrimoniale*), Wernz-Vidal, *Ius Canonicum* (7 vols., in 8, Vol. V, *Ius Matrimoniale,* 3. ed., Romae: apud Aedes Universitatis Gregorianae, 1946) p. 910; Vlaming, *Praelectiones Iuris Matrimonii* (3. ed., 2 vols., Bussum in Hollandia, Vol. 1, 1919, Vol. II, 1921), II, 314; Payen, *De Matrimonio in Missionibus ac Potissimum in Sinis Tractatus Practicus et Casus* (2. ed., 3 vols., Zi-ka-wei: In typographia T'ou-sè-wè, 1935–1936), I, 751 (hereafter cited *De Matrimonio*).

[3] Cf. S. R. R., *Nullitatis Matrimonii,* 27 oct. 1929, coram R. P. D. Henrico

Ordinarily in matters which pertain to the ***bonum publicum*** the confessions of the parties are not accepted as constituting any great degree of certitude. Yet, by the very nature of cases dealing with impotence and non-consummation, these confessions are usually accepted as reliable.[4] Wanenmacher[5] points out that in such cases the Rota has attributed great value to the confessions of the parties in asserting that their marriage had not been consummated. He cites one case in particular, wherein a dispensation was granted when, after sixteen years of married life, the only proof introduced was the *septimae manus* witnesses' corroboration of the confessions of the parties.[6]

The employment of the *septimae manus* witnesses in these particular cases serves a twofold purpose:

1. that they, by their testimony, confirm and corroborate the direct depositions as given by the parties in the case;
2. that they be of help to the court in excluding any possible use of fraud or deceit by the parties.

Since these cases are usually presented to the court by the consorts for the express purpose of acquiring their freedom from the matrimonial bond, the suspicion of possible collusion between the parties is not entirely unfounded. This is particularly the case when both consorts request the dispensation.[7] Therefore, in such circumstances all necessary precautions must be taken to avert the danger of fraud or subornation. The *septimae manus* witnesses, by establishing for the court the moral and religious character of the parties do much to allay the suspicion of collusion in the case.

---

Quattrocolo, dec. LXII, n. 16—*Sacrae Romanae Rotae Decisiones seu Sententiae* (Romae: Typis Polyglottis Vaticanis, 1912—) XXI (1937), 486 (hereafter cited *Decisiones*); S. R. R., *Nullitatis Matrimonii,* 31 mart. 1936, coram R. P. D. Henrico Quattrocolo, dec. XX, n. 3—*Decisiones,* XXVIII (1944), 190.

[4] Cocchi, *Commentarium in Codicem Iuris Canonici ad Usum Scholarum* (8 vols. in 5, Vol. VII, *De Processibus,* 3. ed., Taurinorum Augustae: Marietti, 1940), VII, 477 (hereafter cited *De Processibus*).

[5] *Canonical Evidence,* p. 374.

[6] Cf. S. R. R., *Nullitatis Matrimonii,* 18 augusti 1917, coram R. P. D. Aloisio Sincero, dec. XXIV, n. 3—*Decisiones,* IX (1925), 224-229.

[7] Doheny, *Canonical Procedure in Matrimonial Cases* (2 vols., Milwaukee: The Bruce Publishing Company, 1938-1944), II, 350 (hereafter cited *Canonical Procedure*).

Considered as a proof in these cases the testimony of the *septimae manus* witnesses consists in the sworn statements of seven relatives, friends, or neighbors, introduced by each party to vouch for the credibility of their claims as to the non-consummation of the marriage.[8] These witnesses, fourteen in all, testify under oath that the parties are of an honest and upright character, and that their oath given under such circumstances is worthy of belief.[9] They aver primarily the credibility of the parties in general, and in particular the veracity and the honesty of the spouses concerning the point at issue, that is the non-consummation of the marriage.

### Article 2. *The Nature of the Testimony of the* SEPTIMAE MANUS *Witnesses*

The nature of the testimony of the *septimae manus* witnesses may be classified in three distinct categories:

1. their testimony concerning the general honesty and moral character of the spouses;
2. their testimony concerning the truthfulness and credibility of the latter when they assert that their marriage has not been consummated;
3. their testimony concerning the actual knowledge which they possess in reference to the non-consummation of the marriage.[10]

While the fundamental proof upon which the process of a case involving alleged non-consummation rests is that which is found in the assertions of the parties themselves, these assertions must be confirmed and corroborated before they acquire full juridical

[8] Dolan, *The Defensor Vinculi,* The Catholic University of America Canon Law Studies, n. 85 (Washington, D. C.: The Catholic University of America, 1934), p. 137; Moriarity, *Oaths in Ecclesiastical Courts,* The Catholic University of America Canon Law Studies, n. 110 (Washington, D. C.: The Catholic University of America, 1937), p. 5 (hereafter cited as *Oaths*).

[9] Farrugia, *De Matrimonio et Causis Matrimonialibus Tractatus Canonic-Moralis iuxta Codicem Iuris Canonici* (Taurini, Romae: Marietti, 1924) p. 521, (hereafter cited *De Matrimonio*); Cocchi, *De Processibus,* p. 478; Lanier, *Guide Pratique de la Procédure Matrimoniale en Droit Canonique* (Paris: Pierre Téqui, 1927), p. 24; (hereafter cited *Guide Pratique*); Moriarity, *Oaths,* p. 20.

[10] Payen, *De Matrimonio,* I, 751.

value. Hence it is required by the Code [11] that the religious and moral character of the parties, as well as their credibility, be established by the *septimae manus* witnesses. The Instruction given by the Sacred Congregation of the Sacraments in the year 1923 [12] which is to be followed for the investigating of all cases of non-consummation decrees:

> In his causis, debet uterque coniux testes, qui *septimae manus* audiunt, inducere, sanguine vel affinitate sibi coniunctos, sin minus vicinos bonae fame, aut alioqui de re edoctos, qui iurare possint de ipsorum coniugum probitate, et praesertim de veracitate circa rem deductam in controversiam.[13]

There are to be fourteen witnesses in all, chosen from among the close relations of the parties, or at least from their intimate friends or neighbors.

### Article 3. *The Number of Witnesses Required*

While the term used in description of their office and the nature of their testimony designates the number of witnesses required for the process, this number is not to be considered as determining an iron-clad rule. The Code merely states that these *septimae manus* witnesses are to be supplied,[14] leaving the question of the exact number entirely out of its consideration. All canonists are in accord in stating that it is not absolutely necessary for each party to supply seven such witnesses.[15] When it is impossible to locate

---

[11] Canon 1975, § 1.

[12] S. C. de Sacramentis, decr. *Catholica doctrina* (*De processibus in causis dispensationis super matrimonio rato et non consummato—Regulae servandae—Appendix*), 7 maii 1923—*Acta Apostolicae Sedis, Commentarium Officiale* (Romae, 1909-1929; Civitate Vaticana, 1929—), XV (1923), 389-436. These *Regulae* were separately published by the Vatican Press. A second printing appeared in 1934. This latter printing is the one which is here used, and reference shall be made to it as *Regulae.*

[13] *Regulae,* n. 58.

[14] Cf. canon 1975.

[15] Chelodi, *Ius Matrimoniale,* p. 193; Farrugia, *De Matrimonio,* p. 521; Cocchi, *De Processibus,* p. 478; Cappello, *Summa Iuris Canonici ad Usum Scholarum* (3 vol., Vols. I-II, 3. ed., 1938-1939; Vol. III, 2. ed., 1940, Romae: Apud Aedes Universitatis Gregorianae), III, 386 (hereafter cited

this specified number, a lesser number will be acceptable, provided, however, that reasons are stated as to why the required number was not presented.[16] In the years preceding the Code it was not always necessary that seven such character witnesses be presented.[17] Their number has varied from eleven and fourteen in some instances,[18] to a case in which only one person was presented.[19]

In establishing the norms which are to be followed in these particular cases the Sacred Congregation of the Sacraments stated that seven such witnesses should be supplied by each of the parties,[20] and it is only when it is impossible to present this number, and the reasons why they could not be had are duly listed, that fewer will suffice. The fact that seven from each party is not to be considered as absolutely necessary may be gathered from the Instruction of the Oriental Congregation for such cases. In this Instruction only three character witnesses were demanded for each party.[21]

In a consideration of the number of persons required as character witnesses, the question may be proposed about the possibility of using the same seven witnesses for both the parties. No positive legislation can be found which would cover this particular case, nor do any of the authors discuss it. Frequently it may happen that

---

*Summa*). Payen (*De Matrimonio,* III, 184) stated that three or four such witnesses are sufficient.

[16] *Regulae,* n. 59; Doheny, *Canonical Procedure,* II, 371; cf. S. R. R., *Nullitatis Matrimonii,* 25 iun. 1924, coram R. P. D. Ubaldo Mannucci, dec. XXX, n. 9—" Ex parte vero Friedae testimonium septimae manus deest, sed ratio in actis patet . . ."—*Decisiones,* XVI (1934), 273.

[17] Cf. S. R. R., *Nullitatis Matrimonii,* 15 nov. 1909, coram R. P. D. Gustavo Persiani, dec. XVI, n. 5—*Decisiones* I (1912), 138–139.

[18] S. C. C., *Seinen., Matrimonii,* 15 febr. 1884—*Thesaurus,* CLIII, 147, *ASS,* XVII (1884), 3–15; S. C. C., *Dispensationis Matrimonii,* 14 dec. 1878—*Thesaurus,* CXXXVII, 561, *ASS,* XII (1879), 342.

[19] S. C. C., *Mediolanen., Matrimonii,* 9 aug. 1890—*Thesaurus,* CXLIV, 736; *ASS,* XXIII (1890), 474.

[20] ". . . septem testibus ex utraque parte inductis . . ." *Regulae,* n. 59.

[21] S. C. pro Ecclesia Orientali, *Instructio ad Conficiendos Processus super Matrimonio Rato et non Consummato,* 10 iun. 1935—*AAS,* XXVII (1935), 333–340, " Tres saltem inducat testes, ad normam sacrorum canonum idoneos et omni exceptioni maiores . . ."—*AAS,* XXVII (1935), 336; *Apollinaris,* (Romae; 1928—) VIII (1935), 530.

some of the persons presented to the court are equally familiar with both of the parties.[22] If such a thing should occur and it is evident to the judge that there is no collusion between the parties, or between the witnesses and the parties, their testimony should have great weight. However, if such a practice is followed, the testimony concerning each party should be kept separate, and special mention should be made of this in the acts of the case.

The testimony of the *septimae manus* witnesses is in reality that of character witnesses, and as such these witnesses are to be presented to the court by each of the parties to act as witnesses of credibility.[23] They testify by their oath that the principals are trustworthy and that their oath given under such circumstances can be accepted as reliable.[24] In their testimony the *septimae manus* witnesses swear that they would place absolute credence in the oath given by the spouses that they were not able to consummate their marriage.

The *septimae manus* witnesses offered as an argument of credibility are concerned primarily not with the facts pertaining to the case, but with the moral and the religious character of the consorts,[25] and particularly with the testimony which they have offered.[26] The testimony furnished by the parties themselves and their proper witnesses forms the main body of the proofs,[27] while the *septimae manus* witnesses offer only indirect testimony,[28] which, however, is of use for strengthening the testimony of the parties.[29]

In issuing the various Instructions which are to be followed in

[22] Cf. S. R. R., *Nullitatis Matrimonii,* 27 iun. 1936, coram R. P. D. Stanislao Janasik, dec. XLV, n. 6; " Adest . . . testis Dmã L. D. quae ambas partes iam ante matrimonium noverat." *Decisiones,* XXVIII (1944), 423.

[23] Hickey, " De Processu super Matrimonio Rato et non Consummato—*The Jurist* (Washington, D. C., 1941—), I (1941), 219–220 (hereafter cited as " De Processu ").

[24] Cappello, *Summa,* III, 386.

[25] Doheny, *Canonical Procedure,* II, 372.

[26] ". . . iurati deponant de ipsorum probitate coniugum, et praesertim de veracitate circa rem in controversiam deductam . . ." Wernz-Vidal, V, *Ius Matrimoniale,* p. 911.

[27] Hickey, " De Processu "—*The Jurist* I (1941), 219; *Regulae,* n. 65.

[28] Lanier, *Guide Pratique,* p. 41; Beste, *Introductio,* p. 844.

[29] Canon 1975, § 2.

the investigating of these particular cases [30] the Sacred Congregations have always directed the diocesan tribunals to question the *septimae manus* witnesses concerning the facts of the case. By their testimony in favor of the spouses the *septimae manus* witnesses corroborate the consorts' testimony both directly and indirectly.[31] When they strengthen the testimony of the spouses not only by their character but also by bringing to light some of the facts of the case, the testimony of the *septimae manus* witnesses may be considered as testimony *de credibilitate* and testimony *de scientia.*[32]

### Article 4. *Testimony* DE CREDIBILITATE

Since the fundamental proof upon which the entire process of a declaration of nullity or of a possible dispensation from the bond rests is the assertions of the spouses themselves, these assertions must be confirmed and corroborated before they possess any degree of certitude.[33] Hence it is for this particular purpose that the religious and moral character of the contesting parties must be established, not only by the usual testimonial letters, but even to the extent of calling relatives and friends to bear witness under oath to their credibility.[34] The Instruction of 1923 directs that the consorts produce the so-called *septimae manus* witnesses, who can give sworn testimony to the probity of the parties.[35] They must be in a position to testify whether or not the parties are known to them as religious and honest persons, and whether or not

[30] Cf. S. C. C., instr. *Cum moneat Glossa,* 22 aug. 1840—*Fontes,* n. 4069; S. C. S. Off., instr. *Iudex ad hoc deputatus* a. 1858—*Fontes,* n. 946; S. C. S. Off., instr. (*Ad Ep. Rituum Orient.*) a. 1883—*Fontes,* n. 1076; S. C. Sacr., instr., *Catholica Doctrina,* 7 maii 1923—*AAS,* XV (1923), 389.

[31] ". . . directe quidem dum de inconsummatione se edoctos fuisse declarent tempore non suspecto; indirecte dum actricem fide dignam praedicunt." S. R. R., *Nullitatis Matrimonii,* 16 iun. 1930, coram R. P. D. Iulio Grazioli, dec. XXXVII, n. 15—*Decisiones,* XXII (1938), 416.

[32] Whalen, *Testimonial Evidence,* p. 165.

[33] Hickey, "De Processu"—*The Jurist* I (1941), 217; *Regulae,* n. 58.

[34] ". . . per tale testimonium ipsi redduntur credibiles . . ."—Wernz-Vidal, *Ius Matrimoniale,* p. 910; S. R. R., *Nullitatis Matrimonii,* 21 febr. 1925, coram R. P. D. Ubaldo Mannucci, dec. XIII, n. 7—" Credibilitatem narrationis coniugum firmat testimonium septimae manus . . ." *Decisiones* XVII (1935), 107.

[35] *Regulae,* n. 58.

their oath, when taken under such circumstances, may be accepted as reliable.[36]

The *septimae manus* witnesses are brought in for the purpose of establishing the truthfulness and the probity of the parties,[37] and the character of their testimony, whether favorable [38] or adverse,[39] does not of itself constitute sufficient proof.[40] It is only after it has been confirmed by other corroborative proofs or arguments that it has full juridical value.[41]

The degree of credibility which is to be attributed to the testimony of the *septimae manus* witnesses must always be in proportion to their integrity or probity.[42] Their testimony stands or falls with their own integrity or lack of it. The integrity of the witnesses must always be established through testimonial letters.[43]

---

[36] ". . . partim sive testes credibilitatis sive septimae manus, qui deponunt se coniuges tamquam religiosos et honestos ideoque verisimiliter credere illis coniuges verum dixisse atque juramento confirmasse."—Wernz-Vidal, *Ius Matrimoniale*, p. 294.

[37] Farrugia, *De Matrimonio*, p. 521.

[38] S. R. R., *Nullitatis Matrimonii*, 20 mart. 1926, coram R. P. D. Iulio Grazioli, dec. XI, n. 25—" Testes unanimiter illud etiam affirmant ad quod affirmandum praesertim in causis dispensationis vocantur, actricem nempe eam esse quae plenam mereatur fidem . . ." *Decisiones*, XIX (1935), 88; S. R. R., *Nullitatis Matrimonii*, 2 aug. 1934, coram R. P. D. Francisco Guglielmi, dec. LXXI, n. 10—" Simul testes, ut dicuntur, septimae manus, uncunctanter oratricem praedicant veridicam et periurii incapacem . . ."—*Decisiones*, XXVI (1942), 600.

[39] S. R. R., *Nullitatis Matrimonii*, 25 febr. 1937, coram R. P. D. Henrico Quattrocolo, dec. XV, n. 13— ". . . dum ex adverso vir etiam conventus ab oratricis sorore D. et eius fratre E. praedicatur mendax et capax periurii . . . "—*Decisiones*, XXIX (1945), 156; S.R.R., *Nullitatis Matrimonii*, 5 iun. 1937, coram R. P. D. Andrea Iullien, dec. XLI, n. 11—" Testes autem septimae manus notaverunt Simonem esse hominem qui facile sententiam mutat."—*Decisiones*, XXIX (1945), 407.

[40] Cf. Vermeersch-Creusen, *Epitome Iuris Canonici* (3 vols., Vol. I, 6. ed., 1937; Vol. II, 5. ed., 1934; Vol. III, 5. ed., 1936; Mechliniae-Romae: H. Dessain), III, 131 (hereafter cited *Epitome*) ; *Regulae*, n. 60, 1.

[41] Canon 1975, § 2. Lanier, *Guide Pratique*, p. 25; Doheny, *Canonical Procedure*, II, 373.

[42] Cf. Coronata, *Institutiones Iuris Canonici ad Usum Utriusque Cleri et Scholarum*, (5 vols., Vols. I–IV, 2 ed., 1939–1945; Vol. V, 1936, Romae, Marietti), III, 429 (hereafter cited *Institutiones*) ; Doheny, op. cit. II, 271.

[43] " Allegentur litterae testimoniales quae obtentae sunt circa testium excutiendorum fidem et probitatem."—*Appendix* to *Regulae*, XXVI.

The Sacred Congregation for the Oriental Church requires a more thorough investigation into the character of the parties. Although it accepts the sworn word of the *septimae manus* witnesses to the probity and the veracity of the spouses, it directs that further questions, be asked concerning the facts upon which their opinion in this regard has been based. The judge must question the witnesses about the parties' observance of the ecclesiastical laws and their frequentation of the Sacraments.[44]

This *probatio per testes septimae manus,* as pointed out in the historical treatment, had its origin in the *coiuratores* in the old Germanic Law. It served as the last resort both to dissipate suspicion and to supply for the lack of direct testimony.[45] In the twelfth century this kind of proof was used by the Church as an essential element for the gaining of moral certitude concerning the truth of alleged facts, which on account of their intimate nature were known only to the parties themselves.[46]

The phrase *septimae manus* technically designates the number of witnesses required for the process, while the oath which they take designates the nature of their testimony. They perform their special task of taking the oath of credibility, which is an argument for the veracity of the parties.[47]

The full import of demanding that these witnesses be selected from the relatives and the friends of the parties is apparent from the fact that very frequently they alone are in a position, besides attesting to the general credibility of the parties, to give valuable testimony concerning the pertinent facts of the case.[48] Their character testimony is greatly enhanced when, together with the oath of credibility, they supply a personal knowledge of the facts

---

[44] S. C. pro Ecclesia Orientali, instr. 10 iun. 1935, n. 12: "Testes credibilitatis, praeter ea quae generalia sunt, interrogentur praecipue circa ipsorum coniugum probitatem, vitae honestatem, praeceptorum Ecclesiae observantiam, sacramentorum frequentiam . . ."—*AAS,* XXVII (1935), 336; *Apollinaris,* VIII (1935), 530.

[45] Maschat, *Institutiones Canonicae* (Romae, 1717), Lib. V, tit., 34, n. 5.

[46] C. 5. X, *de frigidis et maleficiatis, et impotentis coeundi,* IV, 15.

[47] S. R. R., *Nullitatis Matrimonii,* 26 mart. 1935, coram Henrico Quattrocolo, dec. XIX, n. 14—". . . at argumentum credibilitatis coniugum recte insuper subministrant ad normam iuris testes septimae manus . . ."—*Decisiones,* XXVII (1943), 177.

[48] Beste, *Instructio,* p. 843.

which is not to be suspected.[49] Under such circumstances they may be classified as witnesses not only *de credibilitate* but also *de scientia.*[50]

## Article 5. *Testimony* DE SCIENTIA

Whenever a marriage case is concerned with the intimate relations of the married life of the spouses, the evidence, as a rule, is very scanty. In such cases only those who have been closely associated with the parties by the close ties of relationship or friendship are in a position to furnish the necessary information. This is precisely the reason why the *septimae manus* witnesses, besides attesting to the honesty and the probity of the spouses, are asked to furnish the more significant facts surrounding their conjugal life.[51]

Most frequently it happens that the close relatives are fairly well acquainted with the private life of the parties. It is not unusual to find a case in which the wife has discussed her marital difficulties with her mother or sister.[52] When such is the case, their testimony in these matters is of paramount importance for the final solution of the case.[53] Worthy of particular notice in this regard, however, is the fact that, before testimony of this type can be constituted as reliable evidence, it must be proved to the satisfaction of the court that these confidences were given *in tempore non suspecto.*

More credence can be placed in the assertions of the spouses if they were made at a time when there were no known reasons for

---

[49] Whalen, *Testimonial Evidence,* p. 166.

[50] "Those who testify that they have learned from the parties or their relatives, at an unsuspected time, that a marriage remained unconsummated, are now known as quasi-ear witnesses (*quasi testes de scientia*)." Wanenmacher, *Canonical Evidence,* p. 115.

[51] Hickey, "De Processu"—*The Jurist,* I (1941), 220.

[52] S. R. R., *Nullitatis Matrimonii,* 20 ian. 1937, coram Henrico Quattrocolo, dec. V, n. 9—"Item deposuit actricis mater: 'Ma confidò anche mia figlia che essa era ancora integra, perchè lo sposo, data la sua debolazza virile, non riusciva a compiere l'atto coniugale.'"—*Decisiones,* XXIX (1945), 35.

[53] Cf. S. R. R., *Nullitatis Matrimonii,* 21 febr. 1925, coram R. P. D. Ubaldo Mannucci, dec. XIII, n. 7—*Decisiones,* XVII (1935), 107; S. R. R., *Nullitatis Matrimonii,* 15 iun. 1923, coram R. P. D. Iulio Grazioli, dec. I, n. 8—*Decisiones,* XV (1932), 7.

concealing the true facts of the case.[54] This element of opportune or non-suspect time must certainly enter into the case. The Sacred Congregation considered it as the time when there was no thought of raising the question for an authoritative decision, and there were no other reasons for concealing the truth or telling a falsehood.[55] If these assertions or extrajudicial confessions were made while the parties were living together [56] or before the marriage took place, the honesty of the parties need not be called into question.

However, if they were made only later, namely, at a time when the domestic life of the parties was being disturbed by serious quarrels or ill feeling, or when there was even a vague notion that the case might be brought into the ecclesiastical court,[57] these confessions are to be considered devoid of all juridical value. For the presumption in such cases is that these assertions were made purely for the sake of deception.[58]

Since the value of these confessions of the parties concerning the details of their married life is limited to cases in which their statements are not inspired or even colored by the hope of gaining a dissolution of the bond, it is easy to understand why the Sacred Congregation of the Sacraments insisted that these confessions must have been given *tempore non suspecto*.[59]

---

[54] Cf. S. R. R., *Nullitatis Matrimonii*, 27 oct. 1929, coram R. P. D. Henrico Quattrocolo, dec. LXII, n. 17—*Decisiones*, XXI (1937), 486; S. R. R., *Nullitatis Matrimonii*, 6 aug. 1934, coram R. P. D. Francisco Guglielmi, dec. LXXI, n. 12—*Decisiones*, XXVI (1942), 600.

[55] " Causam enim valde iuvant partium confessiones extraiudicales tempore non suspecto prolatae; eo nempe tempore, quando de hac questione introducenda ne cogitabatur quidem, nec aliae suberant rationem veritatem occultandi aut falsas proferendi." *Regulae*, n. 70.

[56] Cf. S. R. R., *Nullitatis Matrimonii*, 17 apr. 1926, coram R. P. D. Maximo Massimi, dec. XVII, n. 10—" Ita C. M. testatur se tempore non suspecto a Francisca edoctam fuisse . . . 'Elle m'a dit peu apres son mariage . . .' "—*Decisiones*, XVIII (1935), 136.

[57] Cf. S. R. R., *Nullitatis Matrimonii*, 29 ian. 1937, coram R. P. D. Joanne Teodori, dec. VII, n. 8—*Decisiones*, XXIX (1945), 53; S. R. R., *Nullitatis Matrimonii*, 27 iun. 1936, coram R. P. D. Stanislo Janasik, dec. XLV, n. 6—*Decisiones*, XXVIII (1944), 423.

[58] Doheny, *Canonical Procedure*, II, 392; Wanenmacher, *Canonical Evidence*, p. 161.

[59] *Regulae*, nn. 70; 60, § 2.

When the *septimae manus* witnesses are in a position to give valuable evidence concerning the non-consummation of the marriage they may be rightly classified as *testes de scientia,*[60] and their testimony must not be neglected. Recent Rota decisions have shown that this type of testimony has been most valuable in deciding many cases of this nature.[61] By the Instruction of 1923 the judge is instructed to exercise the greatest diligence in examining the witnesses on these points. He must be most careful in ascertaining just what is the precise origin of their knowledge.[62] It must be accurately determined whence they know these things, when and under what circumstances and from whom they learned them. Was this knowledge acquired by the witness as an eyewitness, or from personal experience, or was it only from the recital of hearsay or from rumor? It is of primary importance to the tribunal that the exact source of this knowledge be determined.[63]

Those who have perceived something with their own sense, i.e., who have first-handed information, are certainly witnesses in the proper sense,[64] and their testimony enjoys excellent credibility.[65]

---

[60] "Testes septimae manus, quatenus sunt de credibilitate, eo maiorem sibi conciliant fidem, quo potiora habent documenta de sua probitate. Habendi sunt autem quasi testes *de scientia,* et hinc maximam faciunt fidem, cum referunt se ex coniugibus aut ex proximioribus parentibus, tempore non suspecto (ut infra, n. 70), didicisse matrimonium mansisse inconsummatum." *Regulae,* n. 60, § 2.

[61] Cf. S. R. R., *Nullitatis Matrimonii,* 20 ian. 1937, coram R. P. D. Henrico Quattrocolo, dec. V, n. 9—*Decisiones,* XXIX (1945), 35; S.R.R., *Nullitatis Matrimonii,* 6 aug. 1934, coram R. P. D. Francisco Guglielmi, dec. LXXI, n. 12—*Decisiones,* XXVI (1942), 600; S. R. R., *Nullitatis Matrimonii,* 23 iun. 1936, coram R. P. D. Henrico Quattrocolo, dec. XLIII, n. 12—*Decisiones,* XXVIII (1944), 408.

[62] *Regulae,* n. 70.

[63] Doheny, *Canonical Procedure,* I, 189.

[64] "Testes de scientia dicuntur illi qui deponunt propria sensu corporea, v. g. visu vel auditu eam perciperunt." Reiffenstuel, *Ius Canonicum Universum,* Lib. II, tit. XX, n. 342.

[65] Cf. S. R. R., *Nullitatis Matrimonii,* 30 dec. 1915, coram R. P. D. Petri Rossetti, dec. XLII, n. 9—*Decisiones,* VII (1924), 469; S. R. R., *Nullitatis Matrimonii,* 16 mart. 1912, coram R. P. D. Michaele Lega, dec. XXIV, n. 3—*Coram Lega Habitae S. R. Rota Decisiones sive Sententiae* (iterum editae, Romae: Typis Polyglottis Vaticanis, 1928), 294 (hereafter cited *Coram Lega Decisiones*).

When a person testifies that he has derived his knowledge from reasoning or conjecture,[66] the judge must inquire just how he arrived at this conclusion; when asked concerning it, the witness is obliged to answer. Witnesses who attest to what they believe took place enjoy no greater credence than the circumstances upon which they have based their testimony.[67]

Hearsay witnesses are, as a general rule, to be rejected. Usually the testimony which they can offer points at best merely to an indication or a presumption of the truth. In each individual case this type of testimony must be evaluated by the judge, for it has proved very valuable in cases wherein the point at issue was very difficult to prove.[68]

When rumor is submitted in the testimony, it is to be given no serious consideration unless it is uniform, constant, and perpetual.[69] Even then before it can have any juridical value, the witnesses must testify that the whole community believed that the fact really existed.[70]

By the Instruction of 1923 the judge is charged with the duty of making certain that those who are best able to give this testimony be cited to appear in court.[71] Relatives are to be chosen, for

---

[66] Cf. Noval, *Commentarium Codicis Iuris Canonici, Lib. IV, De Processibus* (2 vols., Augustae Taurinorum, Romae: 1920–1932), I, 351 (hereafter cited *De Processibus*).

[67] "When a witness testifies that an event is reported to have taken place, the value of his testimony will increase (or decrease) according as the persons named as authors of this repute are grave and reliable and as the causes are probable and proportionate." Wanenmacher, *Canonical Evidence,* p. 162.

[68] S. R. R., *Nullitatis Matrimonii,* 26 febr. 1910, coram R. P. D. Seraphino Many, dec. VIII, n. 9—"Licet plurimi testes qui in causa deposuerunt, sint tantum de auditu, plenam tamen fidem, meretur, tum quia agitur de re, quae in familia notissima erat . . ."—*Decisiones,* II, (1913), 73; S. R. R., *Nullitatis Matrimonii,* 11 dec. 1916, coram R. P. D. Seraphino Many, dec. XXXII, n. 12—*Decisiones,* VIII (1924), 380.

[69] S. R. R., *Nullitatis Matrimonii,* 15 iul. 1911, coram R. P. D. Gulielmo Sebastianelli, dec. XXXI, n. 9—". . . Postremi testes matrimonium non fuisse consummatum dixerunt ex rumore publico, qui circumferebat quaedam turpia viro adscripta, quibus arguebatur eius ad opus coniugale impotentia."—*Decisiones,* III (1915), 344.

[70] Whalen, *Testimonial* Evidence, p. 216.

[71] *Regulae,* n. 66.

it is a valid presumption that close relatives are among the better-informed on the merits of the case.[72]

Domestic servants, neighbors, and close friends can frequently supply valuable information not only regarding the character, but even regarding many of the details surrounding the married life of the spouses.[73] By reason of their dependence upon the parties, the testimony of servants may at times be considered suspect.[74]

Whenever the *septimae manus* witnesses testify concerning their assured knowledge (*de scientia*), the usual rules governing the hearing of witnesses must be observed in the taking of their testimony.[75]

---

[72] This presumption must, however, always yield to the truth. Canon 1747 2.

[73] Cf. S. R. R., *Nullitatis Matrimonii,* 22 iun. 1921, coram R. P. D. Frederico Cattani Amadori, dec. XIV, n. 2—*Decisiones,* XIII (1929), 138; S. R. R., *Nullitatis Matrimonii,* Vic Apost. Tonkin Orientalis, 18 aug. 1921, coram R. P. D. Frederico Cattani Amadori, dec. XXIV, n. 2—*Decisiones,* XIII (1929), 252.

[74] Cf. S. R. R., *Nullitatis Matrimonii,* 19 iun. 1909, coram R. P. D. Gulielmo Sebastianelli, dec. VIII, n. 5—*Decisiones,* I (1912), 70. The judge must determine for the court if this suspicion is well-founded or if it lacks a sound foundation. Cf. Woywod, *A Practical Commentary on the Code of Canon Law* (9th printing, 2 vols. New York: Wagner, 1945), II, 344 (hereafter cited as *Commentary*).

[75] Canons 1756–1791. " Ce sunt les témoins de scientia qui sont produts et entendus suivant les mêmes règles quae pour les affaires de nullitaté de mariage."—Lanier, *Guide Pratique,* p. 41.

# CHAPTER VII

## THE PRESENTATION AND CITATION OF THE *SEPTIMAE MANUS* WITNESSES

### Article 1. *The* SEPTIMAE MANUS *Witnesses Presented by the Parties*

The Code of Canon Law imposes the task of supplying the *septimae manus* witnesses on the parties themselves.[1] These witnesses are introduced in order to corroborate the testimony of the parties by their character testimony, and since it is the character and honesty of the parties that is to be established, the latter must supply these necessary witnesses. Naturally it is expected that they will call upon the various members of their family for this testimony.

Relatives by blood or marriage are ordinarily excluded from offering testimony in contentious cases,[2] because of the presumption that they will allow their relationship either consciously or unconsciously to influence their testimony. Relatives are not infrequently prejudiced in favor of their family, or, because of their strong personal attachments to one another, are able to see only one side of the issue. Notwithstanding the presumption of these suspicions, in matrimonial cases they are to be not only admitted, but their testimony is to be sought. For as Noval (1861–1938) points out, it is a reasonable assumption that their conscience will guide them in their testimony.[3] However, the court must exercise great discretion in hearing their testimony, for the possibility of suspicion against them is not to be entirely disregarded.[4]

In all cases involving non-consummation, each of the parties

[1] Canon 1975 1: ". . . debet uterque coniux testes, qui septimae manus audiunt, inducere . . ."

[2] Canon 1757, § 3.

[3] ". . . non est irrationable confidere quod in re spirituali et adeo gravi timebunt peccare in animan suam . . ." Noval, *De Processibus,* I, 572.

[4] Wanenmacher, *Canonical Evidence,* p. 128.

must be instructed to present to the tribunal the names of seven relatives, friends, or neighbors of good repute.[5] The primary obligation of supplying these witnesses is imposed upon the parties themselves. Since these witnesses are concerned not so much with the facts of the case, their primary purpose being the presentation of testimony affecting the character of the parties, this obligation of presenting them has for its sanction not the invalidity of the process, but merely the loss of credibility for that particular party.[6]

The wording of the Code places this obligation on the parties[7] while the Instruction of 1923 intimates that the judge should request the parties to present the seven names to the court.[8] No matter how the names are presented, whether by the parties of their own accord or at the instance of the judge, these witnesses must be cited according to the regular norms of law.[9]

The Code imposes the obligation of presenting *septimae manus* witnesses only in cases wherein non-consummation has not otherwise been established,[10] and it does not insist upon these witnesses if satisfactory proof can be gained from other sources. Although the Roman Rota has followed the same course and has made recommendations that a dispensation be granted when no such witnesses were presented, the Sacred Congregation of the Sacraments has always been more exacting. The wording of its Instruction for such cases does not tolerate a free choice in the matter. Wanenmacher cites a case in which the Sacred Congregation demanded that the testimony of these character witnesses be included, although the gathering of this testimony was very difficult, as the witnesses lived in a distant diocese.[11] It would seem the wiser practice to introduce them in every case. If, however, the non-consummation is definitely proved by other means, the Rota will not insist upon their presence.

Inasmuch as the establishing of the reliability of the character

---

[5] *Regulae,* n. 58.

[6] Wanenmacher, *Canonical Evidence,* p. 117; Noval, *De Processibus,* I, 572.

[7] Canon 1975, 1: ". . . debet uterque coniux . . . inducere . . ."

[8] *Regulae,* n. 57.

[9] Canons 1715–1723.

[10] Canon 1975.

[11] Wanenmacher, *Canonical Evidence,* p. 118.

of the parties is so necessary for the judgment of the case, both parties must present their proper character witnesses. Should it happen that one of the parties is contumacious and will not appear in court, then his or her character in the matter of reliability still needs to be established. In such a case the petitioner would have the right to make the selection of the necessary character witnesses from among the relatives or friends of the contumacious party.[12] Doheny points out that it is imperative that every possible opportunity of securing the necessary information be employed in compensation for the lack of direct testimony.[13]

### Article 2. *The Witnesses Cited* EX OFFICIO *by the Judge*

Once the Holy See grants the necessary permission, which the validity of the process requires before a non-consummation case can be formally opened,[14] the directing and the conducting of the investigation rests in the hands of the judge who has been duly appointed by the ordinary.[15] It is his duty to conduct the investigation of the facts and to see that they are presented to the Holy See for a final adjudication.[16] In performing his task of conducting the investigation, the judge must follow exactly the norms given by the Sacred Congregation for such a process,[17] and whenever his duties are not therein clearly defined, he must rely upon the general norms governing processes as set forth in the Fourth Book of the Code.[18]

Since the testimony of the parties themselves, given under oath, that their marriage had not been consummated is the chief and

---

[12] *Regulae,* n. 57, § 2.

[13] Doheny, *Canonical Procedure,* II, 363.

[14] Canon 1963, § 1.

[15] Canon 1574; *Regulae,* n. 17, § 1.

[16] The Roman Pontiff in cases concerning two Catholics acts through the agency of the Sacred Congregation of the Sacraments; cf. Canon 1962. If one of the consorts is a non-Catholic, the Holy Office exercises exclusive competence; cf. *AAS,* XX (1928), 75.

[17] "Praesentes regulae in instruendis processibus de non consummatione semper erunt adamussim observandae, et si aliquando ab eis aequa ratio suadeat esse recendedum, iudex de huius rei motivo rationem reddat in actis, ut constet de inobservantiae causae." *Regulae,* n. 99.

[18] Cf. canon 1577, 2; S. C. de Sacramentis, instr. *Pravida*—15 aug. 1936, art. 14, 2—*AAS,* XXVIII (1936), 313; *Regulae,* n. 68.

fundamental proof of the whole process, every care must be taken to establish their credibility. It is precisely for this reason that the judge must cite the *septimae manus* witnesses,[19] in order that they may testify to the good character of the consorts, and in particular to their veracity about the matter now under consideration. The judge must seek to secure very definite and accurate information, and he must not accept vague opinions and surmises. The establishment of the reliability of the character of the principals is under his direction, and the weighing and the judging of the sufficiency of their testimony is in his hands. In the evaluation of the testimony of the *septimae manus* witnesses, however, he must be mindful of the general principles governing the evaluation of testimonial evidence.[20]

If it is a conviction of his that more testimony is necessary, either because of the serious nature of the matter under consideration, or because of the doubtful indications as to the truth of the assertions, he is acting entirely within his power when he demands more proof. The Instruction of 1923 not only allows him, but in case wherein he judges it to be necessary, commands him, to add other witnesses *ex officio* to the *septimae manus* witnesses.[21] In this matter Doheny points out that the judge has very extensive powers to summon these additional witnesses, and that he should not hesitate to call as many as may be required.[22] The judge's powers in regard to such *ex officio* witnesses are enhanced by the Code itself when it states that, when the public good is concerned, he may call *ex officio* as many witnesses as are necessary.[23]

The point at issue is to establish the credibility of the parties. Noval indicated that to establish this point satisfactorily the judge may call *ex officio* those who have been proposed by the *defensor vinculi* or those whom he himself has selected.[24] Whenever either no witnesses at all were designated by the parties, or only a few,

[19] *Regulae,* n. 21.

[20] Canons 1789–1791.

[21] *Regulae,* n. 61.

[22] *Canonical Procedure,* II, 373.

[23] "Sed ipse . . . quoties publicum bonum id exigat, potest testes ex officio inducere."—Canon 1759.

[24] Noval, *De Processibus,* I, 573.

or even when the full quota has been designated but does not suffice to prove the point, the judge must make use of his power to call others *ex officio*.[25]

In the ordinary contentious case, which is concerned only with private affairs, the witnesses together with all the other evidence must be procured by the parties themselves. In such cases the court is not interested in supplying the evidence; the task before the judge is merely to weigh and to evaluate the evidence as it is presented by the parties. However, in affairs which are of vital interest to the public welfare, the court is certainly an interested party. Matrimonial cases, since they deal with the marriage bond, are matters which very intimately concern the public welfare; in such cases the judge must make use of every possible means to ascertain the truth.[26]

While presiding over an ordinary contentious case, whether matrimonial or otherwise, one of the principal duties of the judge is to limit or reduce the number of witnesses so that the trial will not become unduly prolonged.[27] However, in the investigation regarding the non-consummation of a marriage, such is not the case. Instead of eliminating unnecessary witnesses, there is in such an investigation the problem of finding a sufficient number of well-informed persons; as a rule this is a rather difficult task. When those presented to the court prove insufficient to establish the truth of the matter, the judge must try by diligent questions put to the parties to locate additional persons who may be acquainted with the facts of the case. Having done this, he is justified in citing all these witnesses.

The judge must be ever watchful against possible collusion between the parties. At times he may conceive a well-founded suspicion of this when both of the parties agree in requesting the dispensation.[28] They may in a case agree upon a consistent story

---

[25] *Regulae,* n. 61; S. R. R., *Nullitatis Matrimonii,* 25 iun. 1924, coram R. P. D. Ubaldo Mannucci, dec. XXX, n. 9—*Decisiones,* XVI (1934), 272–273.

[26] Woywod, *Commentary,* II, 345.

[27] Canon 1762.

[28] *Regulae,* n. 72.

and present names of witnesses who are in full accord with them. Relatives could very easily be induced to offer false testimony and to testify falsely to the honesty and probity of the spouse. Such character testimony would be pure perjury. [29] If the judge is in any way suspicious that collusion impends, he not only can, but he also must cite sufficient witnesses to counteract the false testimony of the original *septimae manus* witnesses. He can summon them to establish the fact that the principals are not trustworthy, and that their oath in these matters is not reliable and therefore must be rejected.[30]

It is possible, and it certainly does happen, that at times there is collusion between certain witnesses and one of the parties who is attempting to have the marriage set aside. When this is evident and the judge is not satisfied with the character testimony offered for that party, he must call additional *septimae manus* witnesses to establish proof that this particular party is not reliable, and that his or her testimony is not to be accepted.[31] The latter may be able to testify that the moral standards of the party are of such a caliber that he would not hesitate to commit perjury for the sake of entering another marriage. It seems that in such a case wherein the original witnesses are to be rejected, the judge could ask the other party to designate witnesses who would be capable of giving a true estimation of the character of the party.[32]

With reference to the possible cases in which the judge could call these additional *septimae manus* witnesses, it can be stated that he is perfectly free to call them:

1. when a sufficient number of witnesses is not presented to the court by the parties themselves;
2. when no witnesses have been presented for one of the parties inasmuch as he or she is contumacious;

[29] For the penalties imposed by the Church for perjury in a trial, cf. canon 1743, and *Regulae,* n. 40.

[30] Cf. S. R. R., *Nullitatis Matrimonii,* 20 mart. 1926, coram R. P. D. Julio Grazioli, dec. XI, n. 25—*Decisiones,* XIX (1935), 88.

[31] Cf. S. R. R. *Nullitatis Matrimonii,* 28 iul. 1926, coram R. P. D. Francisco Parrillo, dec. XXXIII, n. 11—*Decisiones,* XVIII (1935), 267.

[32] This action is analogous to the procedure which the judge follows when one of the parties is contumacious. Cf. *Regulae,* n. 57, § 2.

3. when there is a suspicion that both parties are trying to deceive the court, and when in consequence thereof their designated witnesses are to be rejected; and
4. when others can be found who can furnish helpful testimony relative to the facts of the case.

## CHAPTER VIII

## PERSONS ACCEPTABLE AS *SEPTIMAE MANUS* WITNESSES

### Article 1. *By Reason of Relationship*

In determining what type of testimony is admissible and in distinguishing between the persons who are capable of offering testimony in the ecclesiastical court, the judge must be ever mindful of the general norms as enacted in the Code. The law has always excluded as completely incompetent those persons whose testimony is likely to be false. The Code expresses the principle that, unless a person is expressly excluded wholly or partially, he can be admitted as a witness.[1] It is the duty of the tribunal to estimate the credibility of each and every witness. In making this evaluation the judge must take cognizance of their natural fitness and their qualification to testify in reference to the nature of the case at hand.[2]

Among the various canons disqualifying a person from acting as a witness the one that is here of prime importance is that by which those who are connected by family ties with the party to the case are excluded. For according to canon 1757 3, § 3,

> "Ut incapaces (repelluntur) coniux in causa sui coniugis, consanguineus et affinis in causa consanguinei vel affinis, in quolibet gradu lineae rectae et in primo gradu collateralis, nisi agatur de causis quae ad statum civilem aut religiosum personae spectant, cuius notitia aliunde haberi nequeat, et bonum publicum exigat ut habeatur."

According to this canon, then, the general canonical principle regards persons as incompetent to act as witnesses in cases involv-

[1] "Omnes possunt esse testes, nisi expresse a iure repellantur vel in totum vel in parte."—Canon 1756.

[2] Whalen, *Testimonial Evidence*, p. 106.

ing their relatives.[3] Nevertheless, in the course of canonical development certain exceptions were always made to this general rule. The reason was that by the exclusion of relatives as witnesses, undue hardships were wrought in matrimonial cases. For it must be considered that relatives, more so than strangers, are qualified to testify in such a case. It is for this reason that this exception to the general law was always considered when the public welfare was concerned.[4] Matrimonial cases, particularly, have a direct bearing on the status of the person involved and are very much concerned with and related to the public welfare; hence, in such cases the testimony of relatives and near-relatives is admis-

[3] Compare the following texts: D. (22.5) 4: "Lege Julia iudicionum cavetur, ne invito denuntietur, ut testimonium litis dicat adversus socerum generum, victrium privignum, sobrinum sobrinam, sobrino sobrina natum, easve qui priore gradu sint, item ne liberto ipsius, liberorum eius, parentium, viri uxoris, item patroni patronae: et ut ne patroni patronae adversus libertas neque liberti adversus patronum cogantur testimonium dicere."

D. (22.5) 5: "In legibus, quibus excipitur, ne gener aut sorer invitus testimonium dicere cogeretur, generi appellatione sponsum quoque filiae contineri placet: item soceri sponsae patrem."

D. (22.5) 9: "Testis idoneus pater filio aut filius patri non est."

C. (4.20) 6: "Parentes et liberi invicem adversus se nec volentes ad testimonium admittendi sunt."

C. 1, C. III, q. 5: "Consanguinei accusatores adversus extraneas testimonium non dicant, nec familiares, vel de domo pradeuntes, sed, si voluerint et invicem consenserint, inter se parentes testificentur, et non in alias."

C. 3, X, *qui matrimonium accusare possunt, vel contra id testari,* IV, 18: "Quod autem parentes, fratres et cognati utriusque sexus in testificatione suorum ad matrimonium coniugendum vel dirimendum admittantur, tam antiqua consuetudine quam legibus approbatur et tam divinis quam humanis legibus adprobatur. Ideo enim maxime parentes recipiuntur, et, si defuerint parentes, proximiores admittuntur, quoniam unusquisque suam genealogiam cum testibus et chartis, tum etiam ex recitatione maiorum scire laborat. Quia igitur aliis melius sciunt, ideo maxime admittuntur. Similiter recipiuntur in testificatione matrimonii gratia coniungendi. Qui enim melius recipi debent, quam illi, quam illi qui melius sciunt, et quorum est interesse, ita, ut, si non interfuerint, et consensum non adhibuerint, secundum leges nullum fiat matrimonium? Quod vero legitur: "pater non recipiatur in causa filii, nec filius in causa patris," in criminalibus causis et contractibus verum est, in matrimonio vero coniungendo et disiungendo ex ipsius coniugi praerogativa, et quia favorabilis res est, congrue admittuntur."

[4] Roberti, *De Processibus,* (2 vols. Romae: Apud Aedes Facultatis Juridicae ad. S. Apollinaris, 1926) II, p. 48, n. 33.

sible, especially in those cases in which the validity of the marriage is being impugned.[5]

This general exception, made for the sake of admitting relatives in order that they may offer testimony, includes all who are related to the spouses:[6] the parents of the parties,[7] and especially the mother of both;[8] the brothers and sisters;[9] and also the aunts and uncles, who like the others are often in a favorable position to furnish valuable information to the court.[10] It is precisely for this reason—that blood relatives are usually more familiar with the domestic problems of the parties—that they are sought out as desirable *septimae manus* witnesses.

In the Germanic law close relatives acted the rôle of this particular type of witness,[11] for it was presumed that they knew the parties better than outsiders. Their relationship increased their credibility, for there was a strong presumption in favor of their veracity and knowledge.[12] A Rota decision formulated shortly

---

[5] Canon 1794; Gasparri, *De Matrimonio,* II, p. 294, n. 1263, Chelodi, *Ius Matrimoniale,* p. 193; Coronata, *Institutiones,* III, p. 196; *Regulae,* n. 58.

[6] Cf. S. R. R., *Nullitatis Matrimonii,* 8 ian. 1921, coram R. P. D. Joanne Prior, dec. I, n. 2—*Decisiones,* XIII (1929), 2; S. R. R., *Nullitatis Matrimonii,* 12 nov. 1921, coram R. P. D. Joanne Priori, dec. XXVIII, n. 3—*Decisiones,* XIII (1929), 264–265.

[7] Cf. S. R. R., *Nullitatis Matrimonii,* 15 iun. 1923, coram R. P. D. Francisco Parrillo, dec. XVI, n. 13—*Decisiones,* XV (1932), 146; S. R. R., *Nullitatis Matrimonii,* 20 ian. 1937, coram R. P. D. Henrico Quattrocolo, dec. V, n. 9—*Decisiones,* XXIX (1945), 35; S. R. R., *Nullitatis Matrimonii,* 16 ian. 1934, coram R. P. D. Francisco Guglielmo, dec. II, n. 10—*Decisiones,* XXVI (1942), 18.

[8] S. R. R., *Nullitatis Matrimonii,* 21 mart. 1936, coram R. P. D. Arturo Wynen, dec. XIX, n. 8—" Mater actricis quae melius omnibus de huismodi re scire deberet . . ."—*Decisiones,* XXVIII (1944), 185.

[9] Cf. S. R. R., *Nullitatis Matrimonii,* 27 oct. 1929, coram R. P. D. Henrico Quattrocolo, dec. LXII, n. 19—*Decisiones,* XXI (1937), 486. S. R. R., *Nullitatis Matrimonii,* 21 ian. 1937, coram R. P. D. Julio Grazioli, dec. VI, n. 13—*Decisiones,* XXIX (1945), 44.

[10] Cf. S. R. R., *Nullitatis Matrimonii,* 10 apr. 1934, coram R. P. D. Henrico Quattrocolo, dec. XVIII, n. 7—*Decisiones,* XXVI (1942), 184.

[11] *Lex Burgundionum,* tit. 8: " Si ingenuus per suspectionem vocatur in culpam . . . sacramentum praebeat cum uxore et filiis et propinquis sibi duodecimus jurent."—*MGH, Leges,* III, 536.

[12] S. R. R., *Nullitatis Matrimonii,* 21 iul. 1910, coram R. P. D. Gulielmo Sebastianelli, dec. XXVIII, n. 5: " Testimonia haec attendenda maxime sunt,

before the Code stated that relatives and friends were never to be overlooked, especially in those cases in which the main points at issue were difficult to prove.[13]

### Article 2. *By Reason of Their Knowledge*

The important task assigned to *septimae manus* witnesses, as previously pointed out, is to establish the credibility of the parties. Most frequently it is not possible to find these witnesses in sufficient number among the relatives. In such cases those who are in no way related to the parties must be called upon to supply this necessary character testimony. After the possibility of drawing these witnesses from the blood relatives and those related by marriage has been exhausted, the Instruction of 1923 offers an alternative norm, namely, " that neighbors of good repute or persons otherwise acquainted with the matter be chosen." [14]

In a consideration of those who are to be accepted as *septimae manus* witnesses from outside the family, some distinctions are appropriate. The knowledge which they possess is the determining factor in their selection, but this knowledge may refer either to the character of the parties or to the facts pertaining to the case.

The possibility or even the probability that one and the same witness may be in a position to supply both character testimony and factual testimony is usually not too remote. Quite frequently it will happen that a neighbor or a friend, besides being able to attest to the credibility of the spouse, is in a position, by reason of confidences which he or she has been given, to give testimony about the intimacies of the conjugal life of the parties.

The question which naturally proposes itself is: What must be done when one and the same witness is not qualified to testify both to the character of the spouse and to the main facts of the case? Should he be rejected for that reason? Is the establishing of the credibility of the parties the main issue, so that a character witness should be chosen, or are the important facts of the case the primary concern?

---

quia consanguinitas non miniut, imo auget fidem, ratione praesumptae scientiae et veritatis."—*Decisiones,* II, (1913), 291.

[13] Cf. S. R. R., *Nullitatis Matrimonii,* 29 iun. 1911, coram R. P. D. Francisco Heiner, dec. XXXVI, n. 4—*Decisiones,* III (1915), 408.

[14] *Regulae,* n. 58.

Hickey is of the opinion that those who can testify only to the general credibility of the parties prove less valuable as witnesses in consequence of being uninformed about the intimacies of their domestic life.[15] The *septimae manus* witnesses are chosen for one purpose. Essentially and basically they are to testify to the credibility of the spouses, for it is the proper characteristic of the testimony of the *septimae manus* witnesses that it furnish an argument for the credibility of the parties of the marriage.[16] The consideration that they may be able to give testimony to the facts of the case is of only secondary import. With reference to these facts the judge has full power to call *ex officio* as many witnesses as he feels are necessary.

Arguments may be drawn from the history of the *septimae manus* witnesses to show that their main function is to establish the credibility of the parties. It was not until 1840 that any mention was made concerning their qualification based on the knowledge of the facts of the case.[17] Until that time they had been employed only with a view to establishing the reliability of the parties.

It is the opinion of the writer that if a choice is to be made between one who can testify to the credibility of the spouses, and another who can depose testimony regarding the more important facts of the case, the character witness is to be preferred as a *septimae manus* witness and the other is to be called by the judge *ex officio* in order that he may act as a witness to the facts in the case.

In formulating the principles which are to govern these cases, the Instruction of 1923, after mentioning relatives both by blood and marriage as available witnesses, states that neighbors and persons otherwise acquainted with the matter are to be called.[18] The Instruction leaves it rather indefinite as to just who, outside of one's kindred, are better suited to act as *septimae manus* wit-

---

[15] Hickey, "De Processu"—*The Jurist,* I (1941), 220.

[16] *Regulae,* n. 71, 1: "Cum proprium sit testimonii septimae manus ut sit argumentum credibilitatis . . ."; cf. Doheny, *Canonical Procedure,* II, pp. 370, 398.

[17] S. C. C., instr. *Cum moneat Glossa,* 22 aug. 1840—*Fontes,* n. 4069.

[18] *Regulae,* n. 58.

nesses. In order to determine more definite norms in this regard it is imperative that some consideration and individual attention be given to those who may serve as possible *septimae manus* witnesses, namely, priests, neighbors, friends, servants, physicians.

*PRIESTS*—It is not rare to find a pastor or priest attesting to the character of one or of both of the parties involved in a matrimonial case.[19] By virtue of canon 1791, § 1, a pastor is considered as a duly qualified witness in a matrimonial case, and as such his testimony is to be considered of the highest value.[20] However, notwithstanding his official capacity as a minister of the Church, when he is called to furnish character testimony, he is acting not as an official minister but merely as a private individual. Acting in this capacity, he is not to be considered as a qualified witness, and hence his testimony in this regard does not constitute complete proof.[21] His testimony, therefore, is devoid of special juridical value, for his attestations amount to an assertion of a mere private opinion or personal observation. Even under such circumstances, and although he does not enjoy the status of an authorized witness in the case, his testimony enjoys great value. When there is a question of supplying character testimony the pastor should never be neglected.[22]

Since a pastor is charged with the religious training of all those who are in his parish, he is expected to be fairly well-acquainted with the religious character of the members of his parish. His position places him in circumstances that enable him to form solid judgments concerning their honesty and probity. The manner in which they observe the laws of the Church and frequent the sacra-

[19] Cf. S. R. R., *Nullitatis Matrimonii,* 20 ian. 1937, coram R. P. D. Henrico Quattrocolo, dec. V, n. 8—*Decisiones,* XXIX (1945), 35; S. R. R., *Nullitatis Matrimonii,* 20 nov. 1937, coram R. P. D. Gulielmo Heard, dec. LXX, n. 14—*Decisiones,* XXIX (1945), 702–703; S. R. R., *Nullitatis Matrimonii,* 12 ian. 1935, coram R. P. D. Ubaldo Mannucci, dec. III, n. 6—*Decisiones,* XXVII (1943), 23; S. R. R. *Nullitatis Matrimonii,* 9 iul. 1929, coram R. P. D. Francisco Morano, dec. XXX, n. 10—*Decisiones,* XXI (1937), 256.

[20] Coronata, *Institutiones,* III, p. 228.

[21] Cf. Canon 1791, § 1; S. R. R., *Nullitatis Matrimonii,* 28 aug. 1911, coram R. P. D. Aloisio Sincero, dec. XXIX, *Decisiones,* III (1915), 439.

[22] Wanenmacher, *Canonical Evidence,* p. 159.

ments forms a foundation for the testimony which he is asked to furnish. The Pastor, then, more than all others, is qualified to testify to the credibility of the members of his parish.

On the other hand, it would indeed be unwise to consider the testimony of the pastor affirming the credibility and trustworthiness of one of the parties as infallible. The evaluation of his testimony and the subsequent evaluation of that of the party does not rest solely upon his recommendation. The court always remains free to make its own appraisal of all testimony including the character testimony of the pastor.[23]

There have been many cases before the Rota in which the testimony of a priest was deemed of little value or of none at all because of some fault of his,[24] or because he was suspected of not being disinterested in the case.[25]

One need not be engaged long in the ministry of the Church before one realizes that by the nature of his office a priest receives many of the confidences of the laity. For the reason that he is a priest many persons seek him out in their troubles and difficulties. He is the recipient of many confidences which the people entrust to him in seeking his counsel. Because of this great trust which has been placed in the priest by the people, the Church has granted priests an exemption from serving as witnesses in canonical trials.[26]

This exemption holds even when the knowledge which they possess has been acquired outside of the confessional but in the exercise of their sacred ministry. The secrets and the confidences which have been committed to them are to be kept inviolable. However, in cases involving non-consummation their testimony is

---

[23] Cf. S. R. R., *Nullitatis Matrimonii,* 17 mart. 1913, coram R. P. D. Antonio Perathoner, dec. XIX, n. 14—*Decisiones,* V. (1919), 224; S. R. R., *Nullitatis Matrimonii,* 30 dec. 1915, coram R. P. D. Ioseph Mori, dec. XLII, n. 15—*Decisiones,* VII (1924), 473–474.

[24] Cf. S. R. R., *Nullitatis Matrimonii,* 20 oct. 1916, coram R. P. D. Gulielmo Sebastianelli, dec. XXIX, n. 4—*Decisiones,* VIII (1916), 329; S. R. R., *Nullitatis Matrimonii,* 27 aug. 1912, coram R. P. D. Michaele Lega, dec. XXXVIII, n. 6—*Decisiones,* IV (1917), 442.

[25] Cf. S. R. R., *Nullitatis Matrimonii,* 17 mart. 1914, coram R. P. D. Aloisio Sincero, dec. X, n. 4—*Decisiones,* VI (1922), 118.

[26] Canon 1755, § 2, 1°; Coronata, *Institutiones,* III, 190; Cocchi, *De Processibus,* IV, 252; Noval, *De Processibus,* I, 327.

to be heard when the public good, the interest of an innocent third party, or the eternal salvation of one of the parties demands it.[27] In these cases they are free and unhampered in disclosing extra-sacramental secrets which may have been committed to them.

As a general rule, when difficulties arise in the conjugal life of parishioners, one of the first to be consulted by the parties is their parish priest. They present to him the facts of the case and await his prudent solution of their problems. This is especially true when it is a case of impotence or non-consummation, for frequently they know of no one else to whom they can safely confide these intimate details. If the priest knows the couple fairly well, he is not taken in by any deceit; and he can readily form a reliable judgment about their truthfulness and the merits of the case.

When a pastor or a priest can, together with his expression of opinion in this matter, testify to facts concerning the non-consummation of a marriage,[28] he must be called upon as a *septimae manus* witness to furnish testimony not only *de credibilitatis* but also *de scientia.*[29] The practice of having a priest furnish this twofold form of testimony is nothing new in the procedural law of the Church. Even in the pre-Code days the testimony of a priest in this regard was considered of high value.[30]

*FRIENDS and NEIGHBORS*—All the various Instructions which enacted norms to be followed in cases of impotence and non-consummation have laid special stress upon the availability of neighbors and friends of unimpeachable reputation as *septimae*

---

[27] Canon 1318, § 1; Vermeersch-Creusen, *Epitome,* II, n. 292; Wernz-Vidal, *De Processibus,* 410; Wanenmacher, *Canonical Evidence,* p. 131.

[28] Cf. S. R. R., *Nullitatis Matrimonii,* 6 aug. 1934, coram R. P. D. Francisco Guglielmi, dec. LXXI, n. 10—*Decisiones,* XXVI (1942), 600; S. R. R., *Nullitatis Matrimonii,* 18 iul. 1911, coram R. P. D. Joanne Prior, dec. XXXII, n. 9—*Decisiones,* III (1915), 351.

[29] S. R. R., *Nullitatis Matrimonii,* 10 mart. 1925, coram R. P. D. Ubaldo Mannucci, dec. XVII, n. 5—*Decisiones,* XVII (1935), 127–128; S. R. R., *Nullitatis Matrimonii,* 25 iun. 1924, coram R. P. D. Ubaldo Mannucci, dec. XXX, n. 9—*Decisiones,* XVI (1934), 272.

[30] Cf. Bassibey, *Le Mariage,* p. 268; Meehan, *Compendium,* p. 273; S. R. R., *Nullitatis Matrimonii,* 18 iul. 1911, coram R. P. D. Joanne Prior, dec. XXXII, n. 9—*Decisiones,* III (1915), 351.

*manus* witnesses.[31] These friends or neighbors, provided that they are cognizant of the marital difficulties in question, may as *septimae manus* witnesses supplant relatives when the latter cannot be provided.[32]

The very first formal Instruction issued by the Sacred Congregation of the Council recognized the importance of the testimony which neighbors are capable of furnishing.[33] Every succeeding Instruction from that time on has insisted that, if relatives could not be present, their place was to be taken by friends or neighbors.

Ordinarily it is relatives that are the first to know of any marital difficulties between the consorts. This, however, cannot be taken as an absolute rule. Many times the parties will seek to keep the members of their families out of their domestic troubles. In such instances it is usually to close friends and neighbors that they turn with their problems. As a general rule, if neighbors know the parties relatively long they usually know the parties quite well and very frequently are well informed of their marital difficulties.[34]

In many of our cities, it is true, a friendly or neighborly spirit is often not in evidence. Notwithstanding this usual aloofness it is quite possible to find some families who are united with each other in close ties of friendship. They are the ones who are to be singled out in the search for *septimae manus* witnesses, for if they know the parties, they can at least attest to their character, or to the standing or reputation that they have in that locality.[35] These neighbors can prove to be quite acceptable witnesses, provided that

---

[31] *Regulae,* n. 58; canon 1975, 1; cc. 5, 7, *de frigidis et maleficiatis, et impotentia coeundi,* IV, 15; S. C. C., instr. *Cum moneat Glossa,* 22 aug. 1840—*Fontes,* n. 4069; S. C. S. Off., instr. *Iudex ad hoc deputatus,* a. 1858—*Fontes,* n. 946; S. C. S. Off., instr. (ad Ep. Rituum Orient.)—*Fontes,* n. 1076.

[32] Payen, *De Matrimonio,* I, 751.

[33] S. C. C., instr. *Cum moneat Glossa,* 22 aug. 1840: "Ut id facilius exequi iudex valeat, defensor matrimonii citabit partem actricem, ut indicet septem, sibi sangquine vel affinitate coniunctos, si fieri possit, sin minus, septem vicinos bonae famae."—*Fontes,* n. 4069.

[34] Doheny, *Canonical Procedure,* II, 370.

[35] Cf. S. R. R., *Nullitatis Matrimonii,* 21 ian. 1937, coram R. P. D. Iulio Grazioli, dec. VI, n. 9—*Decisiones,* XXIX (1945), 42; S. R. R., *Nullitatis Matrimonii,* 20 iun. 1936, coram R. P. D. Guilelmo Heard, dec. XLI, n. 9—*Decisiones,* XXVIII (1944), 389.

they themselves are known to be of good repute, especially in regard to their probity and honesty.[36]

Those who have been friends for a long period of time have no doubt formed many judgments concerning each other's characters; they know just how far and to what extent each may trust the other. They have frequently given and received many mutual confidences; for this reason their testimony in these cases is not only helpful but almost necessary. Their testimony must not be overlooked, for they are often in a position to furnish valuable information which could not otherwise be brought to light.[37]

It should be observed that whenever the parties do not present the names of friends or neighbors to act as *septimae manus* witnesses, the judge should always see to it that at least those who have been on more intimate terms with the parties should be summoned to offer both testimony of character and depositions regarding the facts in the case.

*SERVANTS and DOMESTICS*—One important class which must not be overlooked in the arranging and the eventual citation of *septimae manus* witnesses is that which is comprised of employees and household domestics in the home of the parties. Those who have been constantly associated with the parties in their homes or places of business occupy an advantageous spot from which to form judgments concerning their character and honesty. They know from constant experience, by association with them, to what extent their honesty and truthfulness extends.

Concerning the practice of admitting this particular class of persons as witnesses in canonical trials, Whalen says that it is not possible to delineate general norms applicable in regard to their testimony.[38] By reason of their dependence upon the parties it is

---

[36] Canon 1975, § 1; Cappello, *Summa,* III, 386; Vlaming, *Praelectiones Matrimonii,* II, 314; Payen, *De Matrimonii,* II, 751; Farrugia, *De Matrimonio,* p. 521.

[37] Cf. S. R. R., *Nullitatis Matrimonii,* 2 aug. 1929, coram R. P. D. Maximo Massimi, dec. XLIII, n. 6—*Decisiones,* XXI (1937), 367; S. R. R., *Nullitatis Matrimonii,* 21 ian. 1937, coram R. P. D. Iulio Grazioli, dec. VI, n. 13—*Decisiones,* XXIX (1945), 44; S. R. R., *Nullitatis Matrimonii,* 27 iun. 1936, coram R. P. D. Stanislao Ianasik, dec. XIV, n. 6—*Decisiones,* XXVIII (1944), 423.

[38] *Testimonial Evidence,* p. 136.

possible that at times they may seem to belong to that class of persons who are to be suspected. Although the norms enacted by the Code do not disqualify them from giving testimony, the judge may hold their testimony in suspicion. This would be especially true should there be evidence that their testimony has been colored or influenced to some extent by their devotion or subjection to one of the parties.[39] While at times this may be the case, ordinarily they may be accepted as quite truthful, and their testimony may be considered as excellent in attesting the credibility of the parties.[40]

By reason of their peculiar status in the household it is not expected that servants will have received the confidences of the parties.[41] The knowledge which they possess is usually acquired not from confidences but from observation. A servant living in and caring for the house is in a very excellent position to furnish valuable information concerning the common life of the consorts. The presumption that they are cognizant of what is and has been going on in the house is well-founded.[42]

For example, who more than the one living in the same house would be qualified to testify as to how well the two parties got along with each other, whether they used the same bedroom, whether there were any serious quarrels or ill feelings, and just what were the relations between the contesting parties? Questions such as these certainly have an important bearing on the case. A servant who has been constantly around the house and has taken care of the various needs of the parties can fairly well establish these facts for the court. It is on account of circumstances such as these that the Rota has made it the practice to admit servants as *septimae manus* witnesses when they can furnish information so valuable.[43]

---

[39] Wanenmacher, *Canonical Evidence*, p. 126; cf. S. R. R., *Nullitatis Matrimonii*, 19 ian. 1909, coram R. P. D. Gulielmo Sebastianelli, dec. VIII, n. 5—*Decisiones*, I (1912), 70.

[40] Farrugia, *De Matrimonio*, p. 521.

[41] However, at times such may be the case. Cf. S. R. R., *Nullitatis Matrimonii*, 13 apr. 1935, coram R. P. D. Francisco Guglielmi, dec. XXVII, n. 10—*Decisiones*, XXVII (1943), 245.

[42] Wernz-Vidal, *Ius Matrimoniale*, p. 294.

[43] Cf. S. R. R., *Nullitatis Matrimonii*, 11 apr. 1922, coram R. P. D. Ioanne Prior, dec. XI, n. 5—*Decisiones*, XIV (1930), 95; S. R. R. *Nullitatis Matri-*

Therefore, whenever relatives cannot be had as *septimae manus* witnesses, servants and others in similar positions, if there be any, are not to be neglected.[44] They are generally very well-informed upon those facts upon which the process is essentially based.[45]

*OTHER FACTUAL WITNESSES*—Both the Code and the various Instructions of the Holy See relating to this process make allowances for other witnesses who may be called to testify. After the specific mention of relatives, friends, and neighbors, there is mention of a very general class, namely those who in any other way are acquainted with the matter under consideration, "*alioquin de re edocti.*"[46]

Considering the singular circumstances of individual cases and knowing that no two matrimonial cases are identical, the legislation did not specify any more definite norms concerning these additional witnesses. Further determination was left to the discretion of the judge in the particular case. The judge enjoys very extensive powers in order to guarantee that all persons who are acquainted with the matter under consideration, and all those who in any way can give useful testimony, are not left unsummoned by the court.[47]

The question may be proposed: Are these additional witnesses who are called upon to supply this additional information to be considered as *septimae manus* witnesses? Hickey[48] and Noval,[49] in referring to the summoning of the physicians who have previously examined the parties, state that they are to be included

---

*monii,* 5 febr. 1934, coram R. P. D. Ubaldo Mannucci, dec. V, n. 8—*Decisiones,* XXVI (1942), 43; S. R. R., *Nullitatis Matrimonii,* 15 iul. 1937, coram R. P. D. Iulio Grazioli, dec. LIII, n. 19—*Decisiones,* XXIX (1945), 536; S. R. R., *Nullitatis Matrimonii,* 22 iun. 1921, coram R. P. D. Frederico Cattani Amadori, dec. XIV, n. 2—*Decisiones,* XIII (1929), 137, 138.

[44] Wanenmacher, *Canonical Evidence,* p. 142.

[45] Doheny, *Canonical Procedure,* II, 384.

[46] Canon 1975, § 1; *Regulae,* n. 58; S. C. Sacr., instr. *Provida,* 15 aug. 1936, art. 137—*AAS,* XXVIII (1936), 341.

[47] *Regulae,* n. 62.

[48] "De Processu," *The Jurist,* I (1941), 221.

[49] *De Processibus,* I, 574.

among the *septimae manus* witnesses. Most canonists refer to them only as witnesses to be heard in the case.[50]

In keeping with the principle which has previously been set forth, namely, that the *septimae manus* witnesses are concerned primarily with offering testimony of the credibility of the parties, and only secondarily with offering testimony regarding the facts in the case, it seems that if a person is to testify only to the latter, he does not belong to the category of the *septimae manus* witnesses. At least he would not be a *septimae manus* witness in the true sense of the word. It would be otherwise if he could also attest to the character of the party, and in such case his testimony would be held in high regard by the court.[51] However, when such a person is cited merely to testify to the facts of the case, his testimony will have nothing to do with the character of the party. Wernz (1842–1914)-Vidal (1867–1938) liken them to witnesses who testify to what they have seen or heard, in contradistinction to witnesses of credibility.[52]

The class which is given most frequent mention in this regard by the canonical authors is that which is comprised of physicians who have previously examined the parties when consulted by them.[53]

The canonical examination as conducted by the physicians and experts for cases of impotence and non-consummation is governed by very definite norms of the Code[54] and of the Instruction of 1923.[55] It is beyond the scope of the present purpose to go into

[50] Coronata, *Institutiones,* III, 430; Cocchi, *De Processibus,* p. 483; Beste, *Introductio,* p. 844; Wanenmacher, *Canonical Evidence,* p. 147.

[51] S. R. R., *Nullitatis Matrimonii,* 8 mart. 1924, coram R. P. D. Maximo Massimi, dec. XI, n. 4: Testimonium septimae manus habetur singularis effaciae. Testes enim habentur qui, quasi testes de scientia, maximam faciunt fidem . . ." *Decisiones,* XVI (1934), 88.

[52] ". . . ut testes de visu vel auditu deponunt . . ." Wernz-Vidal, *Ius Matrimoniale,* p. 294; Coronata, *Institutiones,* III, p. 430.

[53] Wernz-Vidal, *Ius Matrimoniale,* p. 294; Hickey, "De Processu," *The Jurist,* I (1941), 221; Hickey, "Requirements of the *Ratum et non Consummatum* Process," *The Jurist,* V (1945), 14; Noval, *De Processibus,* I, 574; Doheny, *Canonical Procedure,* II, 398; Wanenmacher, *Canonical Evidence,* p. 182.

[54] Canons 1976–1982; cf. canons 1792–1802.

[55] *Regulae,* nn. 84–95.

detail in regard to these norms. They are mentioned only on the measure in which they touch upon this particular subject. In conducting any matrimonial process the Church wishes the greatest care to be taken, for the salvation of souls is involved. In the process of nullity arising from possible impotence, in that preliminary to an eventual dispensation in cases of non-consummation, the Church is most careful in the selection of physicians or experts who conduct the physical examination of the parties.

Frequently it happens that when a case of this nature is brought to the attention of the ecclesiastical tribunal, a physician's certificate is also presented. The practice of presenting such a document, although not prescribed by law, does much to save useful time and expense. In the subsequent process of investigating the case before the tribunal, the physicians who have previously examined the parties are excluded from acting as experts in the case,[56] for it is to be feared that they will be unduly influenced by their previous opinion, or prejudiced in favor of the party.[57]

However, a physician who has previously examined only one of the parties is not thereby excluded from conducting the examination of the other; he may also examine the same party in relation to another issue.[58] Although such a one may be excluded from selection by the court for the examination, the benefit of his previous technical knowledge is not to be foregone. He may be called in to act as an ordinary witness regarding the facts in the case or as one stating an opinion.[59] And Doheny points out that the use of the testimony of such a witness is not only permitted but, if it is available, the obtaining of it also becomes obligatory.[60]

All such persons, whether they be physicians, druggists, nurses, obstetricians, or others who are in any way familiar with the facts of the case, are to be considered as good prospects for *septimae manus* witnesses, but only if they are sufficiently acquainted with the parties themselves to be able to testify to their credibility. If

[56] Canon 1978; *Regulae,* n. 88. Their admission, however, would not affect the validity of the process. Cf. Coronata, *Institutiones,* III, 356.

[57] Noval, *De Processibus,* I, 574; Beste, *Introductio,* p. 844.

[58] *Regulae,* n. 88; cf. Doheny, *Canonical Procedure,* II, 446.

[59] *Regulae,* n. 88; cf. Wanenmacher, *Canonical Evidence,* p. 182, Noval, *De Processibus,* I, 574.

[60] *Canonical Procedure,* II, 446.

it is apparent that they have no knowledge concerning the honesty and probity of the parties, they must be considered merely as ordinary witnesses.

Upon due consideration of the admissibility of various persons for the role of *septimae manus* witnesses, it is not amiss to set down some helpful suggestions which may be followed in the selection of these witnesses of credibility.

*Pastors:* The first consideration in any selection of witnesses of credibility should be given to the pastor and to other priests. The molding of religious character and the forming of the traits of honesty and truthfulness is their chief task. By reason of their knowledge of human nature and their positions in life, they are enabled to form solid judgments in this regard. As a rule their testimony enjoys the greatest value in the ecclesiastical court.

*Parents:* Parents have formed very definite ideas as to the traits of honesty and probity of life of their children. They are always interested primarily in seeing that their children do what is right. In the cases here under consideration their testimony is unbiased and desirable.

*Brothers and Sisters:* In the order of availability for the role of *septimae manus* witnesses, brothers and sisters must be preferred after parents, for they know the parties more intimately than all others. As a rule they have been given many confidences in matters which have not been discussed even with the parents.

*Relatives by Blood and by Marriage:* Preference must be given to them by reason of their family connection. Yet, beyond the testimony regarding the character of the parties, frequently they can add nothing.

*Neighbors:* Neighbors give valuable testimony regarding the reputation which the party enjoys within the community. At times they may also be able to supply pertinent facts.

*Friends:* Some friends at least should always be included as *septimae manus* witnesses. They know the parties very well and have given and received many mutual confidences.

*Domestics:* Although the character testimony they are able to offer may at times be rather scanty, they are in a position to supply much information concerning the common life of the spouses.

*Professional men:* Generally these should be employed only as ordinary witnesses. As a rule they cannot testify to the credibility of either party.

# CHAPTER IX

## QUALIFICATION OF THE *SEPTIMAE MANUS* WITNESSES

The admissibility of a person as a witness in any canonical trial is judged basically by the condition of possessing two presupposed qualities. The value of his testimony depends entirely upon the supposition that he has the knowledge required for offering the needed testimony in the case, and that he is perfectly truthful in the presentation of this knowledge to the court.[1]

The first requirement, namely, the knowledge which the witness possesses concerning the matter of the controversy, has been duly considered in the previous chapter. At this point some consideration must be given to his fitness to present this knowledge to the tribunal. All of the disqualifications set up by the Code[2] are based fundamentally upon the inability of the proposed witness to meet these basic requirements. No matter how much knowledge a person may possess, unless it is evident that he will in no way deceive the court in making his statements, his testimony is to be considered as suspect.[3] Such testimony is to be looked upon merely as an indication of the truth,[4] and as a general rule the testimony of such suspected persons is to be wholly excluded from the evidence.[5]

While some persons may be considered completely competent to act as witnesses by reason both of their knowledge and truthfulness, the standards of their profession may hinder them from testifying. Confidences given in the seeking of professional advice and the recipients thereof are, as a general rule, granted immunity in ecclesiastical courts.[6] In the ordinary contentious case this

[1] Wanenmacher, *Canonical Evidence*, p. 119.

[2] Canons 1757–1758.

[3] Wernz-Vidal, *De Processibus*, p. 403.

[4] Noval, *De Processibus*, I, p. 328; Woywod, *Commentary*, II, p. 270.

[5] Canon 1757.

[6] Canon 1755, § 2, 1°.

immunity is upheld and respected. However, in matrimonial cases exceptions are frequently made.

Wanenmacher,[7] in speaking of such confidences, states that in respect to a matrimonial case the public welfare takes precedence over such committed secrets. The public welfare itself excuses these persons from the obligation incumbent upon them by reason of their professional knowledge. Once they have been relieved of this obligation of secrecy, they must testify in court if the public good demands it.[8]

In such cases as these, priests, physicians, nurses and all others who have in any manner shared a secret by reason of their professional standing, may be called upon to testify when the validity of a marriage is being impugned.

One of the means which the Church has at her disposal to offset the possibility of false testimony on the part of witnesses is the oath. By this oath they invoke God to bear witness to what they say.[9] And they promise to give truthful answers to all questions asked of them while they are under oath. Noval felt that if a person were not made conscious of the punishment which is in store for perjury on the side of the divine and human law alike, little hope could be entertained that his assertions would be truthful.[10]

It would, indeed, be an unwarranted assumption to infer that the oath was the sole precaution which the Church takes to assure truthful testimony. If such were the case, the testimony of all those who were prevented from taking the oath, or of those who refused it, would have to be rejected entirely. Even when a person does testify under oath, the oath cannot form the sole criterion of the truthfulness of his statements. By the oath the witness makes himself responsible to God in regard to his truthfulness. The value and the credibility afforded the testimony of witnesses is adjudged not so much by the fact that they have testified under

---

[7] *Canonical Evidence,* p. 131.

[8] Cappello, *Summa,* III, 148; Vermeersch-Creusen, *Epitome,* II, n. 292; Wernz-Vidal, *De Processibus,* p. 411.

[9] Canons 1316, § 1; 1767, § 1; cf. Davis, *Moral and Pastoral Theology,* (4th. ed., London: Sheed and Ward, 4 vols., 1945) II, 44.

[10] Noval, *De Processibus,* II, 338.

oath,[11] but by the proof which has been given concerning their honesty and probity.[12]

In cases involving impotence and non-consummation, the *septimae manus* witnesses testify under oath to the probity and the honesty of the consorts. Credence is gained for their testimony not so much by their oath but by other means. Doheny states that every possible means must be taken to establish the probity and the trustworthiness of every person cited in court.[13] The amount of credence which is given to their attestations must be judged by the evidence of the required qualities of credibility and probity of character. Their testimony stands or falls, not with their having taken or refused the oath, but in relation to their own integrity or the lack of it.[14]

The following question may now be proposed: What value is to be given to the testimony of the *septimae manus* witness who is either prevented from taking the oath or who refuses to do so? Although testimonial evidence loses much of its probative value when not given under oath,[15] is it to be devoid of all juridical value?

The *septimae manus* witness who is prevented from taking the oath is embraced in that class whose testimony the judge is to consider suspect.[16] Since they are deprived of the right to take the oath, it seems that their testimony would be devoid of all value. The very fact that they are to be considered as suspect excludes natural honesty and probity of life as an available argument in favor of their credibility. Since they are already looked upon as suspect, and they cannot take an oath as a means of establishing the truthfulness of their testimony, they lack all credibility. Such

---

[11] The validity of the sentence rendered in a case is not dependent upon the oath taken by the witness. Coronata, *Institutiones*, III, 208.

[12] ". . . leur credibilitate est d'autant plus forte que leur probitate est plus solidement demonstree." A. Villien, "Le Procedure dans les Causes pour Dispense de Mariage non Consumme"—*Le Canoniste* (*Le Canoniste Contemporain*, Paris, 1878–1922; *Le Canoniste*, Paris, 1924–1926, XLVI (1924), 101.

[13] *Canonical Procedure*, II, 271.

[14] Whalen, *Testimonial Evidence*, p. 164; S. C. de Sacramentis, instr. *Provida*, 15 aug. 1936, art. 138—*AAS*, XXVIII (1936), 341.

[15] Noval, *De Processibus*, I, 338.

[16] Canon 1757, § 2.

persons then must be rejected, and they may not be used as *septimae manus* witnesses.

Most of the canonists have adopted the canonical principles, "*testis noniuratus non probat, testi non iurato non creditur.*" The present law, however, makes provisions for cases in which the witness would refuse the oath of telling the truth,[17] and it provides the judge with powers to punish a witness if for no good reason he should thus refuse.[18]

Religious beliefs are most frequently the grounds upon which this refusal is based. Quakers, atheists, and all pagans reject the oath entirely. For atheists and pagans it would be nothing but an empty and meaningless formula. To have such a person take the oath would be to expose the oath to mockery and ridicule.[19] However, such a refusal does not absolutely exclude such a person from acting as a character witness. In cases of non-Catholics, who profess no religious beliefs whatsoever, the judge should obtain from them a solemn promise upon their honor to testify to the truth.[20] Once such a promise has been given, Quakers, atheists and all classes of non-Catholics may be admitted to act in the rôle of *septimae manus* witnesses. Their testimony must be evaluated by the arguments and the witnesses which they can offer for their credibility. It is only when this is the case that such individuals can be admitted for furnishing testimony regarding the character of the parties. Doheny states that both the fact that they have refused the oath together with the reasons for their refusal must be mentioned in the acts.[21]

A more difficult problem arises when it is Catholics who refuse to testify under oath. This is usually a clear indication that they do not intend to give their testimony in a truthful way. If it is clear that this refusal arises from motives of obstinancy, which can readily happen when a witness is cited *ex officio* by the judge to testify to another's character, then the judge would certainly be justified in punishing him for his contumacy.[22] In such a case the

---

[17] Canon 1766, § 2.

[18] Canon 2242, § 2; cf. Whalen, *Testimonial Evidence,* p. 159.

[19] Wernz-Vidal, *De Processibus,* p. 472, nota 3.

[20] Moriarity, *Oaths,* p. 53.

[21] *Canonical Procedure,* II, 314.

[22] Canon 2242, § 2.

refusal of the witness must be mentioned in the acts of the process together with his alleged reasons.[23] Most frequently the reasons which he gives for the refusal will determine his value as a *septimae manus* witness.

It is easy to imagine some Catholics who could feel justified in refusing testimony under oath because of some scruple of conscience. They are persons who would not in the slightest way be tempted to offer false testimony, but because of the tenderness of their conscience may entertain doubts of the absolute truthfulness of their testimony. This situation could very easily arise when such persons are asked, as *septimae manus* witnesses, to give their opinion in regard to the non-consummation of a marriage. Far from showing any disrespect to the court by their refusal of the oath, they would be manifesting their great regard for its sacredness. The judge, in such cases, should try to reason with these individuals and urge them to take the oath. If they persist in their refusal, he should accept their testimony as that of a *septimae manus* witness. The refusal of the oath on such grounds would of itself offer great proof for their credibility. Accordingly their testimony should be evaluated in that light.

Although it cannot be doubted that testimonial evidence loses much of its juridical probative value when not given under oath, unsworn testimony is not to be entirely rejected. When the testimony of the *septimae manus* witnesses is given in this manner, the judge must in each case estimate the degree of credibility which is to be given to their testimony. This he can do by considering the person of the witness, his qualifications to testify, his character and natural traits of honesty together with the testimonials attesting his general credibility. If after such consideration the judgment should be in favor of the witness, his testimony regarding the credibility of the principal party can be admitted.

Quite frequently it happens that one of the parties involved in cases of impotence or non-consummation is a non-Catholic. In

---

[23] S. C. de Sacramentis, instr. *Provida,* 15 aug. 1936, art. 96, 1: ". . . Quod si citatus suas attestationes sub iureiurando reddere renuat, et instructor censeat eas fore utiles ad veritatem detegendam, potest easdem excipere, *facta tamen in actis mentione de iurisiurandi recusatione, eiusque causa."*—*AAS,* XXVIII (1936), 333. (Italics inserted.)

this case it is most likely that the relatives, friends, and neighbors who are presented as *septimae manus* witnesses regarding the character of the non-Catholic party will also be non-Catholics. Is their religious belief to constitute an obstacle which will prevent them from acting as character witnesses?

The testimony of non-Catholics has frequently been admitted in marriage cases,[24] and there is no reason to restrict them from acting as *septimae manus* witnesses. Whenever the non-Catholics are heretics, schismatics, Jews, or any others who profess a belief in God, their testimony must be given under oath.[25]

Non-Catholics as a rule feel that they are under no obligation to appear in the ecclesiastical court. When they do appear and are willing to testify, their religious beliefs must be respected. Wanenmacher[26] allows the judge to hold them under suspicion when canonical prudence warrants it. In practice many non-Catholics can be considered more reliable as witnesses than some Catholics. As long as their character is above reproach there is no reason to exclude them from acting as *septimae manus* witnesses and of offering appropriate character testimony.

[24] Cf. S. R. R., *Nullitatis Matrimonii,* 11 ian. 1912, coram R. P. D. Francisco Heiner, dec. III, n. 6—*Decisiones,* IV (1917), 22; S. R. R., *Nullitatis Matrimonii,* 21 dec. 1912, coram R. P. D. Michaele Lega, dec. XXXI, n. 5—*Coram Lega Decisiones,* 335–336; S. R. R., *Nullitatis Matrimonii,* 23 mart. 1914, coram R. P. D. Gulielmo Sebastianelli, dec. XII, n. 6—*Decisiones,* VI (1922), 146–147.

[25] Moriarity, *Oaths,* p. 53.

[26] *Canonical Evidence,* p. 123.

# CHAPTER X

## THE EVALUATION OF THE TESTIMONY OF THE *SEPTIMAE MANUS* WITNESSES

### Article 1. *Moral Certitude*

For a careful evaluation of the testimony of the *septimae manus* witness it is expedient to consider the degree of certitude which is required on the part of the judge as a basis for his judicial sentence. Concerning the question of certitude and its use in procedure, metaphysical and physical certitude can be immediately eliminated as not required. Nowhere are they demanded by the Code as an indispensable requirement for a judicial decision or sentence. Even the expression "*legitime et certo*" as found in Canon 1069, § 2,[1] which requires that a certain and legitimate proof of nullity or of the dissolution of a prior marriage be obtained before a second union can be permitted, does not, either in its historical background[2] or in the interpretation given it by the modern canonists, demand anything more than moral certitude.[3]

Wernz-Vidal are quite clear in expressing that mere probability is not sufficient, for it does not exclude all prudent doubt.[4] How-

[1] "Quamvis prius matrimonium sit irritum aut solutum qualibet ex causa, non ideo licet aliud contrahere, antequam de prioris nullitate aut solutione *legitime et certo constiterit.*" (Italics inserted.)

[2] Sanchez, *De Matrimonio,* Lib. II, disp. 46, n. 6.

[3] "Absolute certitude is often impossible to obtain and the Church does not exact it, but moral certitude is demanded . . ." Ayrinhac-Lydon, *Marriage Legislation in the New Code of Canon Law* (new revised edition, New York: Benziger Bros., 1932), 131–132 (hereafter cited as *Marriage Legislation*) ; "Certitudo de nullitate aut solutione prioris vinculi moralis sit oportet." Vermeersch-Creusen, *Epitome,* II, 240; Cappello, *Tractatus Canonico-Moralis de Sacramentis,* Vol. III, *De Matrimonio* (4. ed., Taurinorum Augustae: Marietti, 1939), Pars I, p. 487, n. 392 (hereafter cited *De Matrimonio*) ; Chelodi, *Ius Matrimoniale,* p. 89.

[4] ". . . tamen *mera probabilitas,* quae ad *omne dubium prudens* excludendum *non* pertingat, nullo modo sufficit." Wernz-Vidal, *Ius Matrimoniale,* p. 294. (Italics inserted.)

ever, metaphysical or physical certitude is not to be demanded. Rice [5] cites a decision of the Sacred Congregation of the Council in which the *defensor vinculi* was rebuked for insisting on metaphysical rather than moral certitude.[6] By thus excluding the need of metaphysical and physical certitude, and by stressing the insufficiency of mere probability, canonists have followed the middle course and have declared that moral certitude is sufficient.

In all formal ecclesiastical trials, no matter what the nature of the case may be, the judge must always have moral certitude before he is enabled to pass judgment on the merits of the case. Canon 1869 [7] is very explicit in stating this requirement, and in determining what is to be the source from which the judge is to acquire this certitude.

Since certitude may be defined as " the fixed or firm assent or adherence of the mind to the truth, without any prudent fear of error," [8] that moral certitude which excludes every serious and prudent doubt or error, though the possibility of error still remains, is sufficient as a basis for the eventual decision in the case. Even if there were present some slight indication of the opposite's being true, the judge would be justified in passing sentence as long as the proof as seen by him is such as moves prudent men to act in this manner. This doctrine is wholly in conformity with the opinions of the canonists and with the exigencies of human affairs.[9]

---

[5] *Proof of Death in Pre-Nuptial Investigation,* The Catholic University of America Canon Law Studies, n. 123 (Washington, D. C.: The Catholic University of America Press, 1940), p. 106.

[6] S. C. C., *in Mediolanen. Matrimonii,* 22 sept. 1860:—

". . . cum ipse (defensor vinculi), Sacros Canones et Instructionem Sacrae et Universalis Inquisitionis interpretans, tam anxius esset de certitudine omnem penitus oppositi possibilitatem excludente, ut oblivisci videretur, in hoc genere questionum non certitudinem metaphysicam sed moralem certitudinem requiri." Pallottini, *Matrimonium,* Vol. XII, 14, nn. 36–41, 58–64.

[7] Canon 1869, § 1. Ad pronuntiationem cuiuslibet sententiae requiritur in iudicis animo moralis certitudo circa rem sententia definiendam.

§ 2. Hanc certitudinem iudex haurire debet ex actis et probatis.

[8] Coffey, *The Science of Logic* (2 vols., New York: Peter Smith, 1938), II, 211.

[9] " Ad sententiam ferendam certitudo moralis, saltem late dicta, requiritur, id est non quaelibet aeria probabilitas, sed id saltem probabilitatis gradus qui

For all practical purposes canonists admit moral certitude as a governing norm of action in the wide sense rather than simply in the strict and perfect concept which philosophy would attach to this term. It is in the wide sense that certitude is judged sufficient by the Holy See as a means for granting a dispensation which would make possible the celebration of a new marriage in the case of a *matrimonium ratum et non consummatum.*[10]

### Article 2. *Testimony when Taken by Itself*

By far the most important distinction made by the Code concerning proof is that which, with a view to their cogency and effect, divides them into complete or full proofs, and incomplete or partial proof.[11] As the words themselves clearly indicate, full or complete proof definitely manifests the truth of the matter in question, and compellingly moves the mind of the judge to a decision. Partial proof, on the other hand, merely inclines the mind of the judge to one side of the question, the while it leaves the matter still minus its determination.

It is indeed possible in many matrimonial cases that the arguments introduced by both sides of the contention, if considered separately and without contrast to each other, would be considered as affording full proof. However, when these same arguments are considered in view of the proofs alleged by the other side, they may fail to beget sufficient proof to sway the mind of the judge. It is precisely in such cases that the Code authorizes the judge to call for more complete proofs in this particular case.[12]

On the other hand, it is not impossible to find cases in which

negotiis magni momenti omne dubium serium excludit."—Vermeersch-Creusen, *Epitome,* III, 229; " Haec Certitudo moralis non est absoluta et perfecta sed relativa, pro subiecta materia excludens probabilitatem erroris."—Lega-Bartocceti, *Commentarius in Iudicia Ecclesiastica* (3 vols., Romae: Libraria Anonima Cattolica Italiana, 1938–1941), II, 934; Roberti, *De Processibus,* II, 24; Noval, *De Processibus,* I, 409; Coronata, *Institutiones,* III, 317–318.

[10] Boyle, *The Juridical Effects of Moral Certitude on the Pre-Nuptial Guarantees,* The Catholic University of America Canon Law Studies, n. 150 (Washington, D. C.: The Catholic University of America Press, 1942), p. 114.

[11] Cf. canons 1791, § 1, 1835, § 3, 1829.

[12] Canon 1791, § 2.

merely partial proofs, through some added circumstance or presumption, may convince the judge and, as Wanenmacher states, afford the certitude which derives from full proof.[13]

Wernz-Vidal warn against the assumption that partial proofs can be computed arithmetically, as if two partial proofs can be considered as constituting full and complete proof.[14] The Code itself seeks to avoid all gradation and mathematical measurement of proofs. It speaks of those forms of evidence which are to be considered simply as canonical proofs,[15] full proofs,[16] and proofs that are in themselves sufficient,[17] but it adds that more adequate proofs may be demanded for a given case.[18] It also makes mention of some proofs which are to be considered as only partial or semi-plenary proofs,[19] and thus serve simply to lend support to the principal proof.[20]

The testimony of the *septimae manus* witness in cases involving impotence and non-consummation serves primarily to corroborate the testimony of the principal parties.[21] As such it is an argument introduced by the spouses themselves, or called for *ex officio* by the judge, to support the claims of the consorts.[22] Since it offers only indirect testimony[23] of itself, it is not capable of evincing the status of full proof.[24] When witnesses know nothing about the facts of the case, but can merely testify to the good character of the parties, their testimony serves only to corroborate the

---

[13] *Canonical Evidence,* p. 80.

[14] Wernz-Vidal, *De Processibus,* p. 375.

[15] Canons, 1122, § 2; 1454; 1816.

[16] Canons 1791, § 1; 1835, § 3.

[17] Canons 658, § 2; 1791, § 2.

[18] Canons 1791, § 2; 1810.

[19] Canon 1829.

[20] Canons 1758; 1790; 1829; 1975, § 2.

[21] "Testimonium septimae manus est argumentum credibilitatis quod robur addit depositionibus coniugum . . ."—Canon 1975, § 2.

[22] Dolan, *The Defensor Vinculi,* p. 137; Wanenmacher, *Canonical Evidence,* p. 81.

[23] Lanier, *Guide Pratique,* p. 41.

[24] *Regulae,* n. 60; Farrugia, *De Matrimonio,* p. 521; Augustine, *A Commentary on the New Code of Canon Law* (8 vols., Vol. V, 2. ed., St. Louis: Herder, 1920), V, p. 424. (hereafter cited *Commentary.*)

statements made by the parties and cannot of itself produce full proof.[25]

The Code itself deprives such character testimony of full juridical force when it states that it is only when such testimony is confirmed by other admincular indications that it can obtain the force of full proof.[26] As a Canonical proof the testimony of the *septimae manus* witness is by no means peremptory.[27]

The proofs presented in any marriage case can be said to be decisive or conclusive only when they possess sufficient weight in themselves to dispel all prudent doubts which might arise in the mind of the judge. Once all prudent doubts which could beget in his mind the fear of rendering an erroneous decision have been eliminated, he may pass sentence in the case. As long as there remains any doubt he must demand additional proof. For it is only when the weight of the evidence warrants a supreme degree of probability, i.e., such as is exclusive of prudent doubt, that he is justified in making his decision.

The testimony of the *septimae manus* witness, given in substantiation of the assertions of the spouses, cannot as a rule dispel prudent doubt unless, in turn, it is supported by other proofs. Such testimony, then, unless joined with other evidence, is not decisive or peremptory, for it does not tend to prove directly the facts of the case.[28]

When, as it might happen, both of the parties to the marriage concur in requesting the declaration of nullity or a dispensation from the bond, then the suspicion of collusion between the parties is, indeed, well-founded.[29] Unless some more concrete evidence than that furnished by the *septimae manus* witnesses has been introduced, it would be rather difficult to allay this suspicion. As long as the fear of collusion persists, it would be impossible to

---

[25] Woywod, "The Procedural Law of the Code"—*The Homiletic and Pastoral Review,* (New York, 1900—), XXXIV (1934), 53.

[26] ". . . sed vim plenae probationis non obtinet, nisi aliis adminculis aut argumentis fulciatur."—Canon 1975, §2. Cf. Wernz-Vidal, *Ius Matrimoniale,* p. 911.

[27] Chelodi, *Ius Matrimoniale,* p. 193; Cappello, *De Matrimonio,* Pars II, p. 430.

[28] Beste, *Introductio,* p. 844.

[29] Doheny, *Canonical Procedure,* II, 399.

dispel the doubts in the mind of those who are to render a judgment in this particular case.

While it remains true that the primary and basic argument in this process is the moral argument, which is formed by the assertions of the spouses together with the corroborative testimony as furnished by the *septimae manus* witnesses,[30] it is not sufficient in itself to prove the existence of the impediment of impotence or to prove the non-consummation of the marriage.[31] Since such testimony is nothing more than supplementary proof,[32] it carries little weight unless it is substantiated by other types of evidence.

Little or no certitude whatsoever could be had in a case wherein the parties were to disagree concerning the non-consummation of their marriage, if both were to offer *septimae manus* witnesses to corroborate their respective testimonies. It is impossible for both parties to be right. If this type of evidence were to be the only means of proof which could be introduced, such a case would make little or no progress, and would necessarily have to be rejected.

Although the most important argument in these cases generally derives from the *inspectio corporalis*,[33] which indeed can afford the strongest confirmatory proof or argument that can be introduced,[34] yet there are certain instances when an argument of this type would be of little or no value.[35] In these cases, unless more tangible evidence than the testimony of the *septimae manus* witnesses, considered purely as character testimony, could be offered, there would be practically no hope of obtaining a favorable decision in the case.

Although in times past the Church attributed great weight to the

30 Hickey, "The Requirements of the *Ratum et non Consummatum* Process"—*The Jurist,* V (1945), 12.

31 Farrugia, *De Matrimonio,* p. 521.

32 Noval, *De Processibus,* I, 572.

33 Viscont, *Tractatus Canonicus de Matrimonio Rato et non Consummato* (Romae; Apud Ius Pontificium, 1928), p. 50 (hereafter cited *De Matrimonio Rato et non Consummato*).

34 Hickey, "De Processu"—*The Jurist,* I, (1941), 221.

35 This physical examination of the woman would be of little value as a confirmatory proof whenever it had been impossible for the parties to consummate their marriage because there was neither the time, nor the place, nor the opportunity, or when it is certain that the woman is no longer a virgin. Cf. *Regulae,* n. 86.

sworn depositions of the parties when they became substantiated even through the sole testimony of the *septimae manus* witnesses,[36] the present practice is to consider the sworn confessions of the parties as insufficient in view of the interest of the public welfare in the matter.[37] In all cases, then, in which the testimony of the *septimae manus* witnesses is not substantiated by any other evidence, it must be adjudged as of insufficient value in reference to full proof.[38]

### Article 3. *Testimony when Considered along with Other Corroborative Proofs*

Viewed as a corroborative proof the testimony of the *septimae manus* witness has true juridical value, which must not be belittled or overlooked. As corroborative or confirmatory proof, it is to be given preference over all other such arguments, even that argument which results from the physical examination of the parties. In estimating the value of this argument and its relative importance in connection with the physical argument, one must be ever mindful of the exact wording of the Instruction of the Sacred Congregation of the Sacraments.

> ". . . the physical argument . . . is intended to complete the proofs offered by the depositions of the parties and confirmed by the *septimae manus* and other witnesses." [39]

The latest decree from the Holy Office, issued on the 12th of June, 1942, confirms this point. In addition to those cases wherein this physical proof would be futile and useless, it makes provisions for its omission in another case. The decree states

> ". . . the physical examination of the woman could be omitted if in the judgment of the ordinary the fullest

[36] Wanenmacher, *Canonical Evidence*, p. 374.

[37] Viscont, *De Matrimonio Rato et non Consummato*, p. 49.

[38] Cf. *Regulae*, n. 60, 1, in which the wording of canon 1975, § 2, is restated *verbatim*.

[39] ". . . argumentum physicum . . . natum est complere probationem partium confessionem et per testes septimae manus aliosque testes exhibitam."—*Regulae*, n. 65.

> proof has been obtained of the non-consummation in view of the excellent moral qualities of the parties and the witnesses, after all other corroborative arguments had been considered." [40]

In other words, if the ordinary knows with moral certitude the religious character of the parties and of the witnesses, and is confident that they are testifying to the truth in this regard, he may omit the physical examination from the process. Together with the lesser proofs in the case, which proofs serve only as indications or presumptions, the testimony of the *septimae manus* witnesses would justify him in making this decision. If such a practice were to be followed, a notation to that effect should be included in the acts, and special mention made of it in the *votum* of the ordinary.

Hickey [41] points out that the number of instances in which the ordinary will make such a decision will undoubtedly be very infrequent. He doubts if many ordinaries would be willing to shoulder the responsibility for making so important a decision.

Theoretically, the attributing of such probative value to the attestations of the parties and of the *septimae manus* witnesses is indeed a compliment to the religious character of the parties. However, in its practical application, because of the direct bearing which matrimonial cases have on the eternal salvation of the parties, diocesan courts should not be too credulous. Even the most excellent of characters at times may be swayed by passion, and the hope or the intention of contracting another marital union may influence their testimony. In relation to their own marriage, so Doheny states,[42] many otherwise veracious persons would not be fully reliable in their testimony or assertions.

---

[40] S. C. S. Off., instr. 12 iun. 1942— ". . . omitti poterit inspectio si, attenta partium et testium morali excellentia ac serio pensatis eorum animi dispositionibus necnon ceteris adminiculis aut argumentis, ordinarii iudicio, plenissima iam habeatur probatio de impotentia vel de inconsummatione . . ." —*AAS,* XXXIV (1942), 205. For this entire decree and instruction see—Bouscaren, *The Canon Law Digest* (2 vols., Milwaukee: The Bruce Publishing Company, 1934–1943), II, 549–551.

[41] "The Requirements of the *Ratum et non Consummatum Process*"—*The Jurist,* V (1945), 15.

[42] *Canonical Procedure,* II, 371.

Since the decision in such cases is reserved exclusively to the Holy See,[43] and since the diocesan court may in no way decide the case, most of the ordinaries would hesitate to make a judgment dispensing with the physical examination. Before presenting the case to Rome for consideration they would try to present every possible argument as a means of proof. Unless there is a positive obstacle in the way of obtaining this physical proof, most ordinaries would hesitate to proceed in the case without it.

Although only a confirmatory proof in itself, the physical examination so strengthens the testimony of the *septimae manus* witnesses that both arguments together corroborate the assertions of the parties to such a degree that the evidence becomes truly peremptory.

When taken in conjunction with the lesser or minor proofs the *septimae manus* witnesses do not offer the strongest possible evidence. Individually all these minor proofs have only the value of indications or presumptions in favor of the non-consummation of the marriage. However, when viewed as a whole and taken in support of one another, these indications and presumptions are capable of producing weighty evidence. In fact, when the evidence is corroborated by these lesser or adminicular arguments, the testimony of the *septimae manus* witnesses may be considered as truly constituting full proof.[44]

Frequently the causes given for the alleged non-consummation of the marriage will constitute a presumption in its favor.[45] This presumption of itself would not be strong, but when considered with the testimony of the *septimae manus* witnesses, its probative value would be greatly increased. The enumerated causes would most frequently consist in the lack of true matrimonial consent, in force and fear affecting matrimonial consent, in a sudden aversion or hatred on the part of one of the spouses towards the other, and in impotence, whether absolute or relative. The published sentences of the Rota reveal numerous cases which were formally

---

[43] *Regulae,* n. 1.

[44] Cf. Cappello, *De Matrimonio,* Pars II, p. 430, n. 883; Wernz-Vidal, *Ius Matrimoniale,* p. 911; Chelodi, *Ius Matrimoniale,* p. 193; Farrugia, *De Matrimonio,* p. 521.

[45] Wanenmacher, *Canonical Evidence,* pp. 242–243.

tried on one or the other of these counts, and finally were settled by means of a dispensation from a non-consummated union.

In addition to the causes given for the alleged non-consummation of a marriage, Doheny [46] lists many circumstances which, although only indications or presumptions, all help to establish the true facts of the case. If the vast majority of these indications or presumptions point to the non-consummation, it seems that they would be capable of giving great support to the testimony of the *septimae manus* witnesses.

The *septimae manus* witnesses can frequently add great weight to their testimony of credibility when they themselves are in a position to attest to the important facts of the case.[47] When furnishing such evidence they not only serve as character witnesses supporting the claims of the spouses, but they directly confirm their own testimony by means of the knowledge which they have. This twofold type of testimony which they offer has always been looked upon favorably by the Rota.[48]

Among the various proofs which can be used in a case of alleged non-consummation, canonists speak of what they call the *argumentum ex coarctata.*[49] By such an argument they mean that the parties are able to establish the fact that from the time of the marriage ceremony until the present there has been available to them neither the time, the place, nor the opportunity to consummate their marriage. In such cases they are said to have a "continuous alibi." In order that they may make use of such an argument they must be able to produce witnesses or documents which can testify to their whereabouts from the time of the marriage ceremony down to the time of the trial.[50]

The use of such an argument to establish the non-consummation of a marriage will usually occur in relation to those marriages which are contracted either to save the reputation of a girl or to

---

[46] *Canonical Procedure,* II, 420–421.

[47] *Regulae,* n. 60, § 2.

[48] Cf. S. R. R., *Nullitatis Matrimonii,* 27 iun. 1936, coram R. P. D. Stanislao Ianasik, dec. XLV, n. 6—*Decisiones,* XXVIII (1944), 423; S. R. R., *Nullitatis Matrimonii,* 20 ian. 1937, coram R. P. D. Henrico Quattrocolo, dec. V, n. 9—*Decisiones,* XXIX (1945), 35.

[49] De Smet, *Marriage,* I, 219.

[50] Wanenmacher, *Canonical Evidence,* p. 98.

give a name to a child which was conceived outside of lawful wedlock. Technically these marriages are often invalid because of the influence of force and fear, or in view of the lack of true matrimonial consent. However, since it is often practically impossible to establish the invalidity of these counts, a dispensation from a non-consummated union is frequently requested.

The *septimae manus* witnesses cited in these cases are able, as a rule, to testify not only to the character of the parties, but mainly to the fact that the parties involved never lived together, and that the marriage was not consummated after its solemnization.[51] Under such circumstances it seems that the testimony of the *septimae manus* witnesses should be considered more as testimony in the strict sense rather than as testimony of credibility.

---

[51] Cf. Ramstein, *The Pastor and Marriage Cases* (New York: Benziger Bros., 1936), 207.

# CHAPTER XI

## THE USE OF THE *SEPTIMAE MANUS* WITNESSES IN VARIOUS MARRIAGE CASES

### Article 1. *In Cases Wherein Non-Consummation is a Factor*

The type of evidence which is usually sought as proof in a matrimonial case is largely dependent upon the nature of the case under consideration. While public and private documents may form the bulk of evidence in some cases, in others the evidence which they contain would be less valuable. Many cases by their nature preclude the use of documents as evidence.

Because of the intimate details which must be considered in some cases, the parties themselves must be relied upon to furnish the basic proofs. When the subject matter of the case concerns the intimate details of conjugal life, then the parties themselves, as a rule, are the only ones who can furnish this first-hand testimony. All other proofs which are presented in these cases are given only in substantiation of the testimony of the parties themselves. This is particularly true when there is a question of an alleged non-consummated marriage, whether this be the result of impotence or some other reason.

In matrimonial trials, especially those which affect the marriage bond, the assertions of the parties are always heard under oath.[1] By this oath the parties make a solemn profession of the truthfulness of their assertions. Because the fundamental proof in some cases is founded upon the attestations of the parties themselves, additional testimony to their credibility is demanded. This peculiar type of testimony is, for the most part, furnished by the *septimae manus* witnesses. These witnesses afford not only testimony regarding the character of the parties, but also supplementary proof for the case.[2]

Primarily this type of witness is employed in those cases in

[1] Cf. Canon 1744.

[2] Noval, *De Processibus,* I, 572.

which the validity of a marriage is impugned on grounds of impotence on the part of one of the parties. Most cases of impotence lie in the category of functional impotence, which is extremely difficult to prove by means of the physical examination as conducted by experts. Unless this physical examination can furnish concrete evidence as to the presence of the impediment and its existence at the time of the marriage, the *septimae manus* witnesses must be used. In such cases they may testify not only to the credibility of the parties, but they may even furnish direct evidence to establish the existence of the impediment.[3]

Quite frequently it happens that it is impossible to obtain conclusive proof of the existence of the impediment at the time of the marriage. Many such cases which are at first introduced on the grounds of impotence are eventually settled by means of a dispensation granted by the Holy See from a non-consummated union.

According to the latest Instruction from the Holy See for the conducting of such cases,[4] the employment of the *septimae manus* witnesses is necessary in all cases which are being investigated with the hope that the non-consummation of the marriage may be demonstrated.[5] The Code had demanded and insisted upon their presence only in those cases in which the presence of the impediment or the fact of non-consummation could not be proved by other means.[6] Since the validity of the dispensation from a non-consummated union is contingent upon the twofold facts

1. That the non-consummation of the marriage has been duly established; and
2. That the causes alleged are true;

the *septimae manus* witnesses must be able to testify to both of

[3] E.g. Witnesses have testified that they had known for many years that the man involved in the case was impotent. Cf. S. R. R., *Nullitatis Matrimonii,* 10 mart. 1925, coram R. P. D. Ubaldo Mannucci, dec. XVIII, n. 5—*Decisiones,* XVII (1935), 129.

[4] S. C. de Sacramentis, instr. 7 maii 1923—*AAS,* XV (1923), 389-436.

[5] *Regulae,* n. 58: "In his causis, debet uterque coniux testes, qui septimae manus audiunt, inducere . . ."

[6] Cf. Canon 1975, § 1, "In causis impotentia ve inconsummationis, *nisi impotentia vel inconsummatione aliunde certo constet,* debet uterque coniux testes, qui septimae manus audiunt, inducere . . ." (Italics inserted).

these points. Canonical authors, while they discuss at great length the proofs for non-consummation and the necessity of true causes for the dispensation, all fail to make any mention of questioning the *septimae manus* witnesses concerning the existence of valid causes. Although this is not mentioned in so many words by the Instruction, it is certainly a justifiable inference.[7] Therefore, no matter how conclusive the evidence may be in favor of the alleged non-consummation, it is not permitted to omit the questioning of the *septimae manus* witnesses.

Of this type of case would be many of those marriages which are ratified at a much later date than their celebration. Such would be the case in regard to a *matrimonium legitimum*,[8] if both of the contracting parties were to receive the sacrament of baptism subsequent to their marriage. After the reception of baptism by the second party the marriage would become what canonists are accustomed to speak of as a *matrimonium consummatum et ratum non-consummatum.* It would be possible to obtain a papal dispensation from this union. In such a case it would be necessary to prove conclusively that the marriage was not consummated after its ratification, and the existence of a valid cause. Wanenmacher in speaking of such a case states that the proof necessary in the case would be the documentary evidence to show that the separation took place before the baptism of the second party together with the supplementary oaths of both parties corroborated by the *septimae manus* witnesses.[9]

### Article 2. *In Cases Involving Consent*

The practice of employing *septimae manus* witnesses in cases investigated on other counts had long been abolished, even before the promulgation of the Code of Canon Law. During the last century these witnesses were cited in other cases which were

---

[7] The *septimae manus* witnesses are supposed to establish the veracity of the consorts about the subject matter of the controversy—*Regulae* n. 58; mention has been made of this point in the sample questionnaire as supplied by the Instruction, *Appendix,* XXII.

[8] "Matrimonium inter non baptizatos valide contractum dicitur legitimum." —Canon 1015, 3; cf. Cappello, *De Matrimonio,* Pars II, p. 58, n. 47.

[9] Wanenmacher, *Canonical Evidence,* p. 98.

difficult to prove and which were lacking in conclusive evidence.[10] This indiscriminate use of such witnesses was prohibited in consequence of an interpretation given by the Holy Office which stated that *septimae manus* witnesses were to be used only in those cases wherein the consummation of the marriage was in question.[11]

While Wanenmacher mentions them as opinion witnesses which may be employed also in cases of insanity and duress,[12] other canonists mention their use only in cases of impotence and non-consummation.[13] In regard to their use in other cases, especially those dealing with the defect of matrimonial consent, the Rota has repeatedly pointed out that they are not to be used.[14]

While it is necessary that the religious character of the parties always be established in matrimonial trials, the *septimae manus* witnesses are permitted to perform this task only in cases involving impotence and non-consummation.

---

[10] The *septimae manus* witnesses were employed in an effort to establish the lack of consent in a *vis et metus* case—S. C. C., *Calven et Theanen.*, 26 iun. 1869—*Fontes*, n. 4214—*Thesaurus*, CXXVII, 343; and to establish the impediment of affinity arising from previous illicit intercourse—S. C. C., *Gesnen. et Posnanien.*, 9 sept. 1894—*Thesaurus*, CLIII, 1302.

[11] S. C. S. Off., 16 febr. 1894—*ASS*, XXVII (1894), 153; cf. Gasparri, *De Matrimonio*, II, p. 295, n. 1264.

[12] *Canonical Evidence*, p. 116.

[13] Cf. Wernz-Vidal, *Ius Matrimoniale*, pp. 294, 910; Cappello, *De Matrimonio*, Pars. II, 261; Lega, *De Iudiciis*, IV, 461; Chelodi, *Ius Matrimoniale*, p. 193; Moriarity, *Oaths*, p. 5.

[14] Cf. S. R. R., *Nullitatis Matrimonii*, 6 iun. 1935, coram R. P. D. Maximo Massimi, dec. XLIII, n. 6—*Decisiones*, XXVII (1943), 365; S. R. R. *Nullitatis Matrimonii*, 21 dec. 1923, coram R. P. D. Maximo Massimi, dec. XXV, n. 13—*Decisiones*, XV (1932), 318.

# APPENDIX I

## A QUESTIONNAIRE FOR THE *SEPTIMAE MANUS* WITNESSES

The law of the Church places very special safeguards around the method of putting questions to the witnesses. The formulation of the actual questions for the case at hand is a task assigned to the *defensor vinculi.* A prepared list of questions must be submitted by him which are to be enclosed in an envelope, sealed with the seal of the *curia,* and are opened and read only by the court in the act of the examination.[1] These questions must be prepared for the individual witnesses and enclosed in separate envelopes. The questions both in their matter and form must be in conformity with the requirements of law.[2]

Because no two particular matrimonial cases are identical, especially cases dealing with impotence and non-consummation, no predetermined set of questions can be used in all cases. The *defensor vinculi* must formulate specific questions for each particular case. In formulating his questions he must remember that they are to be framed so as to indicate that these witnesses are primarily character witnesses, attesting to the credibility of the party on whose behalf they have been called.[3]

A formulary of questions based upon the following sample of a questionnaire seems adequately to include all the points which necessarily must be considered in the examination of the *septimae manus* witnesses.

### QUESTIONNAIRE FOR THE *SEPTIMAE MANUS* WITNESSES

1. What is your name?
2. What is your father's name and your mother's maiden name?

---

[1] Canon 1968; Sipos, *Enchiridion Iuris Canonici* (Pecs: Ex Typographia "Haladas R. T.," 1926), p. 878; Coronata, *Institutiones,* III, p. 421.

[2] Cf. Canon 1775; Sipos, *Enchiridion Iuris Canonici,* p. 845.

[3] Dolan, *The Defensor Vinculi,* p. 138.

3. When and where were you born?
4. How old are you?
5. Where do you live?
6. What means of identification have you?
7. What is your business or occupation?
8. What is your religion?
9. Do you practice it faithfully?
10. What is the name of your parish and your pastor?
11. How long have you known————?
12. Are you a relative of————?
13. If so, what is the degree of your relationship?
14. On what occasion did you first come to know————?
15. What is his (her) religion?
16. Does he (she) practice it faithfully?
17. Can you testify to the religious character and honesty of ————?
18. Do you think that he (she) has told the truth?
19. Do you think that he (she) is capable of committing perjury in this matter, if it would be to his (her) advantage?
20. Would you be willing to accept his (her) word in this regard?
21. When and where were these parties married?
22. How long did they live together?
23. Do you know whether the parties entered this marriage of their own free will and mutual love?
24. What signs of mutual love did they manifest before their marriage?
25. What signs did they manifest after their marriage?
26. Do you know whether they occupied the same room and slept together?
27. Did they make any attempt to consummate their marriage?
28. If so, were they successful in this attempt?
29. When did you first learn that the marriage had not been consummated?
30. Did either of the parties ever mention this matter to you?
31. If so, which one and when?
32. Was this matter mentioned to you before they separated?

33. Did either one of them ever mention to you the possibility of seeking a dissolution of their marriage?
34. When was this possibility first mentioned to you?
35. What reasons did they give for the alleged non-consummation of their marriage?
36. Was it due to any hatred or antipathy between the parties?
37. Was either of the parties impotent?
38. Were any remedies used to overcome this impotence?
39. Was medical advice sought by either of them in this regard?
40. What means did they use to overcome this impediment?
41. Was the professional advice which they sought helpful?
42. When did the parties separate?
43. How long had they lived together?
44. What was the cause given for this separation?
45. What was the attitude of the parties towards each other after their separation?
46. Have they been in the company of each other since then?
47. If so, how often and on what occasions?
48. What is your personal judgment in regard to the asserted non-consummation of this marriage?
49. What is the common opinion in the estimation of others as to this alleged non-consummation?
50. Do you know of others who have knowledge of this matter, and who could furnish additional testimony in this case?
51. Do you know when the petitioner first thought of seeking a dissolution of this marriage?
52. When and how did they learn of the possibility of obtaining such a dissolution?
53. Would you think that it is possible to effect a reconciliation between the parties?
54. What causes would they give for the granting of such a dispensation?
55. Do you consider these causes as being true?
56. If so, why?
57. Have you anything to add, omit, correct or change in this testimony?
58. Would you be willing to take an oath that you believe the

spouses to be truthful when they testify under oath that their marriage was not consummated? [4]

---

[4] This formulary has been compiled from the samples of questions as found in: *Regulae, Appendix,* XXVII; Doheny, *Canonical Procedure,* II, 386–388; Wanenmacher, *Canonical Evidence,* pp. 152–153; Lanier, *Guide Pratique,* p. 71; Laboure-Byrnes, *Procedure in the Diocesan Courts of First Instance* (New York: Benziger Bros., 1928) pp. 181–184; Cappello, *Praxis Processualis ad normam Codicis et peculiarium S. Sedis Instructionum* (Romae: Marietti, 1940), pp. 127–128.

## APPENDIX II

## CASES CONCERNING THE NULLITY OF SACRED ORDINATION

While it is quite true that cases dealing with the nullity of Sacred Ordination are not common in our diocesan tribunals, on rare occasions such actions are introduced in them. The Church has made ample provisions for the instituting of such a process not only by establishing the ordinary norms of law as embodied in the Code,[1] but also my means of a special Instruction which was issued by the Sacred Congregation of the Sacraments in 1931.[2]

Cases petitioning for the freedom from the obligations attached to Sacred Orders are reserved to the Holy See.[3] The Sacred Congregation of the Sacraments enjoys sole competence over them; diocesan courts may investigate these particular cases only as delegates of the Holy See.

After the introductory *libellus* has been received, the Holy See decides whether the case is to be tried according to regular court procedure or in the so-called disciplinary form. If the decision is in favor of the former, the local ordinary is then delegated to try the case before his diocesan tribunal.[4] In the investigation of these cases the special regulations enacted for the process followed in matrimonial cases are to be applied together with their necessary adaptations.[5] At the termination of the inquiry the tribunal, as the court delegated by the Holy See, is empowered to pass a definite sentence upon the merits of the case.[6]

---

[1] Canons 1993-1998.

[2] S. C. de Sacramentis, instr. 9 iun. 1931—*AAS,* XXIII (1931), 457; Bouscaren, *The Canon Law Digest,* I, 812-832.

[3] Canon 1993.

[4] Such cases must be tried before a collegiate tribunal, consisting of three judges. Cf. canon 1576, 11.

[5] Ea omnia, quae tum in Sectione Prima huius Partis, tum in peculiari titulo de processu in causis matrimonialibus sunt dicta, servavi etiam debent, congrua congruis referendo, in causis contra sacram ordinationem—Canon 1995.

[6] Woywod, *Commentary,* II, 351.

If the Holy See favors the disciplinary form of action, the conduct of the trial is quite different. The case is remanded to the local tribunal which institutes a process to obtain the information for the Sacred Congregation of the Sacraments, which reserves to itself the final decision and judgment on the case. The process which is followed in this instance is that set forth on the decree and in the Instruction which was issued by the Sacred Congregation for cases concerning the nullity of Sacred Ordination or the obligations inherent in Sacred Orders.[7]

Many of the rules incorporated in this Instruction were taken almost word for word from the previous Instruction of the same Congregation for the investigation of cases of the alleged non-consummation of a marriage.[8] Since a detailed commentary upon the function of the *septimae manus* witnesses as set forth in this latter Instruction would involve a repetition of nearly the entire contents of this work, this will not be attempted. Comparisons and comments will be made upon this function as found in the Instructions, and references will be given to the respective article of both. Only those articles of both Instructions which deal with the subject matter at hand, i.e., the *septimae manus* witness, will be considered.

Article 45 of the Instruction of 1931 states that before the examination of the plaintiff is completed, he is to be asked to produce witnesses who can testify to the fact that he lacked the proper intention, or to the presence of compulsion, or any other defect which might have affected his consent. These witnesses are to be chosen from his family or from those familiar with his family affairs, because they are probably able to furnish useful testimony.[9] Witnesses from this category are presumed to be better acquainted with the facts of the case. Although they may have an interest in the case by reason of their relationship, they are to be admitted in all cases which pertain to the religious or civil status of the party concerned.[10]

---

[7] S. C. de Sacraments, instr. 9 iun. 1931—*AAS,* XXIII (1931), 457.

[8] S. C. de Sacramentis, instr. *Catholic Doctrina,* 7 maii 1923—*AAS,* XV (1923), 392–436.

[9] Cf. *Regulae,* n. 57.

[10] Canon, 1757, § 3, 1°.

One important difference which must be noted in the witnesses called for by the two Instructions is that the witnesses cited in Ordination cases are primarily employed in the demonstration of the facts of the case. For this reason Cappello calls them "*quasi testes de scientia.*"[11] On the contrary, in the process involving non-consummation of marriage they are interested primarily in establishing the religious and moral character of the spouses and in giving testimony to their credibility.[12] Although interested primarily in the all-important facts of the case, witnesses cited in a process concerning ordination must also certify to the character of the petitioner and especially to his veracity in regard to the point in controversy.[13] They are to be called upon to establish his moral integrity and to help the court in ascertaining whether or not his testimony is to be considered reliable.[14]

Testimony which is given to the character of a party is never capable of producing full proof, for it is only an argument of credibility,[15] and it must not be considered as anything more than supplementary proof.[16] It is only when it is substantiated by other types of evidence of a more direct type that it is peremptory.[17] When the witnesses cited in an Ordination case can testify that they have learned from the plaintiff or his family *in tempore non suspecto* that he did not have the intention of receiving Sacred Orders or that he explicitly excluded the acceptance of their obligations, they are entitled to the fullest belief and must necessarily be considered as direct witnesses.[18]

The close parallel between cases investigating the validity of Ordinations and those investigating the alleged non-consummation

---

[11] *Tractatus Canonico-Moralis de Sacramentis,* Vol. II, Pars III, *De Sacra Ordinatione* (Romae: Marietti, 1935), p. 633. (hereafter cited *De Sacra Ordinatione*).

[12] Supra, page 86.

[13] S. C. de Sacramentis, instr. 9 iun. 1931, art. 46, 1—*AAS,* XXIII (1931), 467.

[14] Cf. *Regulae,* nn. 58–60.

[15] Canon 1975, § 2.

[16] Noval, *De Processibus,* I, 572.

[17] Chelodi, *Ius Matrimoniale,* p. 193; cf. *supra,* p. 169.

[18] S. C. de Sacramentis, instr. 9 iun. 1901, art. 46, 2—*AAS,* XIII (1931), 467–468; cf. *Regulae,* n. 60, 2.

of a marriage is ample justification for following the practice of the Roman Rota in treating cases of the latter type. When *septimae manus* witnesses are in a position to testify to the all-important facts pertaining to the case, this testimony has been looked upon as strong confirmatory proof of their character testimony. Therefore, when they not only support the claims of the parties by their testimony concerning their credibility, but bring to light first-hand information which they possess, their testimony is to be considered as having excellent value.[19] If, then, in a case concerning the validity of Sacred Orders or the obligations inherent therein, the witnesses supply not only the indirect testimony to the character of the plaintiff, but also to the lack of the intention of the plaintiff at the time of his ordination, their testimony is entitled to the fullest credit.[20]

Witnesses who are cited *ex officio* by the judge can greatly influence the eventual outcome of the case. As a rule, when a party is requested to produce witnesses for the court, it is only natural that he should present those who are favorably inclined towards his cause. Since cases which concern the civil or religious status of an individual have a direct bearing upon the common good, it is the duty of the judge to make sure that adequate proof is presented to the court.[21] In cases dealing with Sacred Ordination or the acceptance of its obligations, unless the truth is made sufficiently apparent by the witnesses presented to the court, the judge must call additional ones.[22] This is particularly true when indications are found in the testimony submitted that there are additional persons who can furnish valuable testimony.[23] It happens frequently that former classmates of the cleric or friends associated with him before his ordination may be able to furnish

---

[19] Cf. S. R. R., *Nullitatis Matrimonii,* 27 iun. 1936, coram R. P. D. Stanislao Janasik, dec. XLV, n. 6—*Decisiones,* XXVIII (1944), 423; S. R. R., *Nullitatis Matrimonii,* 20 ian. 1937, coram R. P. D. Henrico Quattrocolo, dec. V, n. 9—*Decisiones,* XXIX (1945), 35.

[20] S. C. de Sacramentis, instr. 9 iun. 1931, art. 46, 2—*AAS,* XXIII (1931), 467, 468.

[21] Canon 1759, § 3.

[22] S. C. de Sacramentis, instr. 9 iun. 1931, art. 46, 3—*AAS,* XXIII (1931), 468.

[23] *Regulae,* n. 62.

valuable information concerning the intention of the plaintiff. These witnesses should never be left unsummoned no matter how clear and concise the evidence at hand may be.

The actual examination of these witnesses is subject to the general norms of procedure as set forth in the Code.[24] If an important witness cited by the court is prevented from appearing, a notation to this effect must be made in the acts of the case,[25] so that it may be made clear to the Sacred Congregation that no apparent source of proof was neglected or left unchecked.

After examination upon the various points which have an intimate bearing upon the merits of the case, and before his dismissal, the witness should have read to him the testimony given by the plaintiff at whose suggestion he was cited. Then he is to be asked whether or not he considers these statements made by the plaintiff as worthy of belief.[26]

It seems to be within the rights of the judge to cite not only those witnesses who may support the claims of the plaintiff, but especially those who may testify to his unreliability.[27] Since the whole case is founded upon deception practiced by the plaintiff either at the time of his ordination or at the time of the opening of the case, the presumption is in favor of his unreliability. This presumption should form the basis for the cross-examination of the witnesses by the defender of Sacred Orders.[28]

When witnesses have testified to anything which directly affects the merits of the case, the exact source of this knowledge must be clearly described. It is necessary that a clear distinction be made between private information, gained directly from the plaintiff or his intimates, and that which is mere rumor or hearsay. It is the duty of the court to ascertain whence, how, and where the witnesses acquired this knowledge.

---

[24] Canons 1770–1781.

[25] S. C. de Sacramentis, inst. 9 iun. 1931, art. 49—*AAS,* XXIII (1931), 468; *Regulae,* n. 26.

[26] S. C. de Sacramentis, 9 iun. 1931, art. 51, 1—*AAS,* XXIII, (1931), 468; *Regulae,* n. 68, § 1.

[27] Cf. S. R. R., *Nullitatis Matrimonii,* 20 mart. 1926, coram R. P. D. Iulio Grazioli, dec. XL, n. 25—*Decisiones,* XIX (1935), 89.

[28] S. C. de Sacramentis, instr. 9 iun. 1931, art. 51, 2—*AAS,* XXIII (1931), 468–469; *Regulae,* n. 68, § 2.

The element of unsuspected time (*tempus non suspectum*) must be given heed in the case. The confessions made by the plaintiff are considered valuable only when they are made at a time when there was no reason for concealing the truth or for telling a falsehood.[29]

[29] Compare *Regulae,* n. 70, and *ibid. art.* 53—*AAS,* XXIII (1931), 469. Cf. supra, p. 51.

# CONCLUSIONS

The following conclusions have been drawn from this study of the *septimae manus* witnesses and the testimony which they offer.

1. In matrimonial cases the *septimae manus* witnesses may be used either by the party to establish his credibility and thus to corroborate his statements, or by the court to discredit the statements made by the party by attesting to his unreliability.
2. If the judge is not satisfied with the original witnesses, he may *ex officio* call additional *septimae manus* witnesses to counteract the testimony of those presented by the parties.
3. Since the testimony of the *septimae manus* witnesses is enhanced or decreased according to their own probity, their reliability must be thoroughly established either by testimonial letters of their pastor or by character testimony given by other reliable persons.
4. Unless a person can offer testimony concerning the character of the party, no matter how much he can contribute to the case, he should not be cited as a *septimae manus* witness. Aside from the possibility of offering testimony regarding the character of the party, he should rather be cited as a witness in the strict sense.
5. Although the canonical authors neglect to mention the questioning of the *septimae manus* witnesses in regard to the existence of a valid cause for a dispensation, it is imperative that they be questioned upon this point.
6. While the Code demands their presence only in cases wherein the impediment of impotence or the non-consummation of a marriage can not otherwise be proved, the Instruction of 1923 demands that the testimony of the *septimae manus* witnesses be had in every case of alleged non-consummation.

# BIBLIOGRAPHY

## SOURCES

*Acta Apostolicae Sedis, Commentarium Officiale,* Romae, 1909–1929; Civitate Vaticana, 1929 —.

*Acta Sanctae Sedis,* 41 vols., Romae, 1865–1908.

Bouscaren, T. Lincoln, *The Canon Law Digest,* 2 vols., Milwaukee: The Bruce Publishing Company, 1934–1943.

*Codex Iuris Canonici Pii X Pontificis Maximi iussu digestus Benedicti XV auctoritate promulgatus,* Romae: Typis Polyglottis Vaticanis, 1917.

*Codicis Iuris Canonici Fontes,* cura Emi Petri Card. Gasparri editi, 9 vols., Romae (postea Civitate Vaticana): Typis Polyglottis Vaticanis, 1923–1939. (Vols. VII–IX ed. cura et studio Emi. Iustianiani Card. Seredi.)

*Coram Lega Habitae S. R. Rotae Decisiones sive Sententiae,* iterum editae, Romae: Typis Polyglottis Vaticanis, 1928.

*Corpus Iuris Canonici,* ed. Lipsiensis secunda post Aemilii Richteri curas instruxit Aemilius Friedberg, 2 vols., Lipsiae: Ex Officina Bernhardi Tauchnitz, 1879–1881. Editio anastice repetita, Lipsiae: Tauchnitz, 1922.

*Decretales D. Gregorii Papae IX suae integritati una cum glossis restitutae, cum privilegio Gregorii XIII, Pont. Max., et aliorum Principum,* Romae, 1582.

Instructio S. C. de Sacramentis, *Catholica Doctrina,* Regulae Servandae in Processibus super Matrimonio Rato et non Consummato, 7 maii 1923, ed. altera, Typis Polyglottis Vaticanis, 1934.

Jaffé, P., *Regesta Pontificum Romanorum ab condita Ecclesia ad annum post Christum natum MCXCVIII,* 2. ed., cura Wattenbach, Kaltenbrunner, Ewald, Loewenfeld, 2 vols. in 1, Lipsiae, 1885–1888.

Mansi, Ioannes, *Sacrorum Conciliorum Nova et Amplissima Collectio,* 53 vols. in 60, Parisiis, 1901–1927.

*Monumenta Germania Historica, Leges,* 5 vols., ed. G. Pertz, G. Waitz, H. Brunner, Hannoverae, 1835–1889.

*Monumenta Germaniae Historicae, Legum Sectio II, Capitularia Regum Francorum,* 2 vols. ed. A. Boretius, Hannoverae, 1883–1893.

Pallottini, Salvator, *Collectio omnium conclusionum et resolutionum quae in causis propositis apud Sacram Congregationem S. Concilii Tridentin Interpretum prodierunt ab eius institutione anno MDLXIV ad annum MDCCCLX,* 17 vols., Romae, 1868–1893.

Potthast, Augustus, *Regesta Pontificum Romanorum inde ab anno post Christum natum MCXCVIII ad annum MCCCIV,* 2 vols., Berolini, 1874–1875.

*S. R. Rotae Decisiones seu Sententiae,* Romae: Typis Polyglottis Vaticanis, 1912—.

Schroeder, H. J., *Canons and Decrees of the Council of Trent, Original Text with English Translation,* St. Louis: Herder Book Co., 1941.

*Thesaurus Resolutionum Sacrae Congregationis Concilii,* 167 vols., Romae, 1718–1908.

## REFERENCE WORKS

Augustine, Charles, *A Commentary on the New Code of Canon Law,* 8 vols., Vol. V, 2. ed., St. Louis: Herder, 1920.

Ayrinhac, H. A., *Marriage Legislation in the New Code of Canon Law,* revised and enlarged by P. J. Lydon, New York: Benziger, 1932.

Barbosa, Augustinus, *Collectanea doctorum, tam veterum quam recentiorum, in ius pontificium universum,* 6 vols., in 5, Lugduni, 1716.

Bassibey, R., *Le Mariage devant les Tribuneaux Ecclésiastiques,* Paris, 1899.

Berardi, Carolus, *Gratiani Canones Genuini ab Apocryphis Discreti,* 3 vols. in 4, Venetiis, 1777.

Beste, Udalricus, *Introductio in Codicem,* Collegeville, Minn.: St. John's Abbey Press, 1938.

Boyle, David, *The Juridical Effect of Moral Certitude on the Pre-Nuptial Guarantees,* The Catholic University of America Canon Law Studies, n. 150, Washington, D. C., The Catholic University of America Press, 1942.

Bouix, M. D., *Tractatus de Judiciis Ecclesiasticis,* 3. ed. 2 vols., Parisiis, 1883.

Bücher, Karl, *The Roman Law Contract,* London, 1895.

Brunner, Henrich, *Deutsche Rechtsgeschichte,* 2. ed., 2 vols., edited C. von Schwerin, Munchen und Leipzig: Verlag von Duncker & Humblot, 1928.

Cappello, Felix, *Summa Iuris Canonici in Usus Scholarum,* 3 vols., vol. I-II, 3. ed., 1938–1939; Vol. III, 2. ed., 1940; Romae: Apud Aedes Universitatis Gregorianae.

*Tractatus Canonico-moralis de Sacramentis,* Vol. III, Pars I & II, *De Matrimonio,* 4. ed., Taurinorum Augustae, Romae; Marietti, 1939; Vol. II, De Sacra Ordinatione, Taurinorum, Augustae, Romae; Marietti, 1935.

*Praxis Processualis ad normam Codicis et peculiarium S. Sedis Instructionum,* Romae: Marietti, 1940.

Chelodi, Ioannes, *Ius Matrimoniale iuxta Codicem Iuris Canonici,* e. ed., Tridenti: Libr. Edit. Tridentum, 1921.

Cocchi, Guidus, *Commentarium in Codicem Iuris Canonici,* 8 vols. in 5, Vol. VII, *De Processibus,* e. ed., Taurinorum Augustae: Marietti, 1940.

Coronata, Mattheus Contea, *Institutiones Iuris Canonici ad Usum Utriusque Cleri et Scholarum,* 5 vols., Vols. I–IV, 2. ed., 1939–1945; Vol. V, 1936.

Coffey, P., *The Science of Logic,* 2 vols. New York: Peter Smith, 1938.

Davis, Henry, *Moral and Pastoral Theology,* 4 vols., 4. ed., London: Sheed and Ward, 1945.

De Becker, Iulius, *De Sponsalibus et Matrimonio,* 2 ed., 2 vols., Lovanii, 1903.

De Smet, *Betrothment and Marriage,* 2. ed., 2 vols. St. Louis: Herder, 1925.

Dill, Samuel, *Roman Society in Gaul in the Merovingian Age,* London: Macmillan, 1926.

Doheny, William, *Canonical Procedure in Matrimonial Cases,* 2 vols., Milwaukee: The Bruce Publishing Company, 1938–1944.

Dolan, John, *The Defensor Vinculi,* The Catholic University of America Canon Law Studies, n. 85, Washington, D. C.: The Catholic University of America, 1934.

Duchesne, L., *Le Liber Pontificalis,* 2 vols., Paris, 1886–1892.

Engel, L., *Collegium Universi Juris Canonici,* 4 vols. in 1, Venetiis, 1760.

Esmein, A., *Le mariage en droit canonique,* deuxieme edition mise a jour par R. Genestal et J. Dauviller, 2 vols., Paris: Recueil Sirey, 1929–1935.

———, *A History of Continental Criminal Procedure,* Vol. V of the Continental Legal History Series, Boston: Little, Brown & Co., 1927.

Farrugia, Nicholas, *De Matrimonio et Causis Matrimonialibus Tractatus Canonico-Moralis iuxta Codicem Iuris Canonici,* Taurini, Romae: Marietti, 1924.

Feije, Henricus, *De Impedimentis et Dispensationibus Matrimonialibus,* 3. ed., Lovanii, 1885.

Freisen, Joseph, *Geshichte des canonischen Eherechts bis zum Verfall de Glossenlitteratur,* 2. Ausgabe, Paderborn, 1893.

Gasparri, Petrus, *Tractatus Canonicus de Matrimonio, ed.* nova ad mentem Codicis I. C., 2 vols. in 1, Romae: Typis Polyglottis Vaticanis, 1932.

Glasson, E., *Histoire du Droit et des Institutiones de la France,* 7 vols., Paris, 1889.

Gregoire de Tours, *Histoire de Francs,* 2 vols., nouvelle edition, Paris: René Poupardin, 1913.

Gregory of Tours, *History of the Franks,* trans. by O. M. Dalton, 2 vols., Oxford: The Clarendon Press, 1927.

Hefele, Carolus, et Leclercq, Henricus, *Histoire des Conciles,* 10 vols., in 19, Paris: Libraire Letouzey et Ané, 1907–1938.

Hinschius, Paulus, *Decretales Pseudo-Isidorianae et Capitula Angilramni,* Lipsiae, 1863.

Hostiensis, Cardinalis (Henricus de Segusia) *In Quinque Decretalium Libros Commentaria,* 5 vols., in 3, Venetiis, 1581.

———, *Summa Aurea,* Venetiis, 1570.

Joyce, George, *Christian Marriage,* London: Sheed and Ward, 1933.

Kerin, Charles, *The Privation of Christian Burial,* The Catholic University of America Canon Law Studies, n. 136, Washington, D. C.: The Catholic University of America Press, 1941.

Laboure, Theodore and Byrnes, William, *Procedure in the Diocesan Courts of First Instance,* New York: Benziger Brothers, 1928.

Lanier, Henri, *Guide Pratique de la Procédure Matrimoniale en Droit Canonique,* Paris: Pierre Tequi, 1927.

Lega, M., *Praelectiones de Iudiciis Ecclesiasticis,* 4 vols., Romae, 1896–1901.

Lega, M. Bartoccetti, V., *Commentarius in Iudicia Ecclesiastica iuxta Codicem Iuris Canonici,* 3 vols., Romae: Anonima Libraria Cattolica Italiana, 1938–1941.

Lingard, John, *The Antiquities of the Anglo-Saxon Church,* Philadelphia, 1841.

Meehan, A., *Compendium Juris Canonici,* Roffae, 1899.

Migne, J. P., *Patrologiae Cursus Completus, Series Latina,* 221 vols., Parisiis, 1844–1864.

Moriarity, Eugene, *Oaths in Ecclesiastical Courts,* The Catholic University of America Canon Law Studies, n. 110, Washington, D. C.: The Catholic University of America, 1937.

Maschat, R., *Institutiones Canonicae,* Romae, 1717.

Noval, Joseph, *Commentarium Codicis Iuris Canonici, Lib. IV, De Processibus,* 2 vols. Augustae Taurinorum, Romae, 1920–1932.

Payen, G., *De Matrimonio in Missionibus ac Potissimum in Sinis Tractatus Practicus et Casus,* 2. ed., 3 vols., Zi-Ka-wei: in typographia T'ou-sè-wè, 1935–1936.

Pirhing, E., *Jus Canonicum in Quinque Libros Decretalium Distributum Nova Methodo Explicatum,* ed. novissima, 5 vols. in 4, Dilingae, 1722.

Ramstein, M., *The Pastor and Marriage Cases,* New York: Benziger Brothers, 1936.

Rice, Patrick, *Proof of Death in the Pre-Nuptial Investigation,* The Catholic University of America Canon Law Studies, n. 123, Washington, D. C.: The Catholic University of America Press, 1940.

Roberti, F., *De Processibus,* 2 vols., Romae: Apud Aedes Facultatis Juridicae ad S. Apollinaris, 1926.

Rufinus, *Summa,* edited by von Schulte, Giessen: Verlag von Emil Roth, 1892.

Sanchez, Thomas, *Disputationum de Sancto Matrimonii Sacramento Libri Tres,* Antverpiae, 1626.

Sanguinetti, Sebastianus, *Iuris Ecclesiastici Privati Institutiones,* Romae, 1884.

Schmalzgrueber, F., *Ius Ecclesiasticum Universum,* 5 vols. in 12, Romae, 1843–1845.

Smith, *Elements of Ecclesiastical Law,* 3. ed., 3 vols., New York, 1888.

Sipos, Stephanus, *Enchiridion Iuris Canonici,* Pecs: Ex Typographia "Haladas R. T.," 1926.

Van Espen, Z., *Ius Ecclesiasticum Universum Ceteraque Scripta Omnia,* 5 vols., Venetiis, 1769.

Vermeersch, A.,-Creusen, J., *Epitome Iuris Canonici,* 3 vols., Vol. I, 6. ed., 1937; Vol. II, 5. ed., 1934; Vol. III, 5. ed., 1936; Mechliniae-Romae, H. Dessain.

Viscont, Antonius, *Tractatus Canonicus de Matrimonio Rato et non Consummato,* Romae: Apud Ius Pontificium, 1928.

Vlaming, Th., *Praelectiones Iuris Matrimonii ad Normam Codicis Iuris Canonici,* 3. ed., 2 vols., Bussum in Hollandia, 1919–1921.

Wanenmacher, Francis, *Canonical Evidence in Marriage Cases,* Philadelphia, The Dolphin Press, 1935.

Wernz, Franciscus, *Ius Detretalium,* 6 vols., Romae et Prati, 1898–1905.

Wernz, F.,-Vidal, P., *Ius Canonicum,* 7 vols. in 8, Romae: Apud Aedes Universitatis Gregorianae, 1928–1946. Vol. I, 1938, Vol. II, 3. ed., 1943; Vol. III, 1933; Vol. IV, Pars I, 1934; Vol. IV, Pars II, 1935; Vol. V, 3. ed., 1946; Vol. VI, 1928; Vol. VII, 1937.

Whalen, Donald, *The Value of Testimonial Evidence in Matrimonial Procedure,* The Catholic University of America Canon Law Studies, n. 99, Washington, D. C.: The Catholic University of America, 1935.

Woywod, Stanislaus, *A Practical Commentary on the Code of Canon Law,* 9th printing, 2 vols., New York: Wagner, 1945.

## PRINCIPAL ARTICLES

———, " Regulae Servandae in Processibus super matrimonio rato et non consummato " and " S. Congregatio pro Ecclesia Orientali Instructio ad conficiendos processus super matrimonio rato et non consummato "—*Apollinaris,* VIII (1935); 501–549.

Hickey, J., " De Processu super matrimonio rato et non consummato."—*The Jurist,* I (1941), 210–224.

Hickey, J., " The Requirements of the *ratum et non consummatum* Process."—*The Jurist,* V (1945), 1–19.

Villien, A., " La Procedure dans les Causes pour Dispense de mariage non consummé." *Le Canoniste,* XLVI (1924), 49–64, 97–112.

Woywod, S., " Procedural Law of the Code."—*The Homiletic and Pastoral Review,* XXXIV (1933–1934), 53–62.

## PERIODICALS

*Apollinaris,* Romae, 1928—.

*Canoniste, Le,* Paris, 1924–1926 (originally *Le Canoniste Contemporain,* Paris, 45 vols., 1878–1922.

*Homiletic and Pastoral Review, The,* New York, 1900—.

*Jurist, The,* Washington, 1941—.

## ABBREVIATIONS

*AAS—Acta Apostolicae Sedis*

*ASS—Acta Sanctae Sedis*

*Decisiones—S. S. Rotae Decisiones seu Sententiae*

*Fontes—Codicis iuris canonici fontes cura Emi Petri Card. Gasparri editi*

Jaffé—*Regesta Pontificum Romanorum ab condita Ecclesia ad annun post Christum natum MCXCVIII*

Mansi—*Sacrorum conciliorum nova et amplissima collectio*
*MGH—Monumenta Germaniae Historica*
*Regulae—Regulae Servandae in processibus nato et non consummato*
S. C. C.—Sacra Congregatio Concilii
S. C. S. Off.—Suprema Congregatio Sancti Offici
S. R. R.—Sacra Romana Rota
*Thesaurus—Thesaurus Resolutionum Sacrae Congregationis Concilii*

## ALPHABETICAL INDEX

## BIOGRAPHICAL NOTE

Timothy Joseph McNicholas was born on November 18, 1917, at Chester, Pennsylvania. He attended St. Robert's Parochial and High School of that city. In September of 1935 he was admitted in St. Gregory's Preparatory Seminary, Cincinnati, Ohio. After theological studies at Mount Saint Mary of the West, Norwood, Ohio, he was ordained to the Holy Priesthood on June 6, 1943. In September of the following year he enrolled in the School of Canon Law of the Catholic University of America, where he received the degree of the Baccalaureate in Canon Law in May of 1945, and the degree of the Licentiate in Canon Law in June of 1946.

## Canon Law Studies *

1. Freriks, Rev. Celestine A., C.PP.S., J.C.D., Religious Congregations in Their External Relations, 121 pp., 1916.
2. Galliher, Rev. Daniel M., O.P., J.C.D., Canonical Elections, 117 pp., 1917.
3. Borkowski, Rev. Aurelius L., O.F.M., J.C.D., De Confraternitatibus Ecclesiasticis, 136 pp., 1918.
4. Castillo, Rev. Cayo, J.C.D., Disertacion Historico-Canonica sobre la Potestad del Cabildo en Sede Vacante o Impedida del Vicario Capitular, 99 pp., 1919 (1918).
5. Kubelbeck, Rev. William J., S.T.B., J.C.D., The Sacred Penitentiaria and Its Relation to Faculties of Ordinaries and Priests, 129 pp., 1918.
6. Petrovits, Rev. Joseph J. C., S.T.D., J.C.D., The New Church Law on Matrimony, X-461 pp., 1919.
7. Hickey, Rev. John J., S.T.B., J.C.D., Irregularities and Simple Impediments in the New Code of Canon Law, 100 pp., 1920.
8. Klekotka, Rev. Peter J., S.T.B., J.C.D., Diocesan Consultors, 179 pp., 1920.
9. Wanenmacher, Rev. Francis, J.C.D., The Evidence in Ecclesiastical Procedure Affecting the Marriage Bond, 1920 (Printed 1935).
10. Golden, Rev. Henry Francis, J.C.D., Parochial Benefices in the New Code, IV-119 pp., 1921 (Printed 1925).
11. Koudelka, Rev. Charles J., J.C.D., Pastors, Their Rights and Duties According to the New Code of Canon Law, 211 pp., 1921.
12. Melo, Rev. Antonius, O.F.M., J.C.D., De Exemptione Regularium, X-188 pp., 1921.
13. Schaaf, Rev. Valentine Theodore, O.F.M., S.T.B., J.C.D., The Cloister, X-180 pp., 1921.
14. Burke, Rev. Thomas Joseph, S.T.D., J.C.D., Competence in Ecclesiastical Tribunals, IV-117 pp., 1922.
15. Leech, Rev. George Leo, J.C.D., A Comparative Study of the Constitution "Apostolicae Sedis" and the "Codex Juris Canonici," 179 pp., 1922.
16. Motry, Rev. Hubert Louis, S.T.D., J.C.D., Diocesan Faculties According to the Code of Canon Law, II-167 pp., 1922.
17. Murphy, Rev. George Lawrence, J.C.D., Delinquencies and Penalties in the Administration and the Reception of the Sacraments, IV-121 pp., 1923.

* All published numbers are available from the Catholic University of America Press, 621 Michigan Ave., N.E., Washington 17, D. C., except the following numbers: 1-114 inclusive, and numbers 116, 118, 120, 122, 123, 162 and 198.

18. O'Reilly, Rev. John Anthony, S.T.B., J.C.D., Ecclesiastical Sepulture in the New Code of Canon Law, II-129 pp., 1923.
19. Michalicka, Rev. Wenceslas Cyrill, O.S.B., J.C.D., Judicial Procedure in Dismissal of Clerical Exempt Religious, 107 pp., 1923.
20. Dargin, Rev. Edward Vincent, S.T.B., J.C.D., Reserved Cases According to the Code of Canon Law, IV-103 pp., 1924.
21. Godfrey, Rev. John A., S.T.B., J.C.D., The Right of Patronage According to the Code of Canon Law, 153 pp., 1924.
22. Hagedorn, Rev. Francis Edward, J.C.D., General Legislation on Indulgences, II-154 pp., 1924.
23. King, Rev. James Ignatius, J.C.D., The Administration of the Sacraments to Dying Non-Catholics, V-141 pp., 1924.
24. Winslow, Rev. Francis Joseph, M.M., J.C.D., Vicars and Prefects Apostolic, IV-149 pp., 1924.
25. Correa, Rev. Jose Servelion, S.T.L., J.C.D., La Potestad Legislativa de la Iglesia Catolica, IV-127 pp., 1925.
26. Dugan, Rev. Henry Francis, A.M., J.C.D., The Judiciary Department of the Diocesan Curia, 87 pp., 1925.
27. Keller, Rev. Charles Frederick, S.T.B., J.C.D., Mass Stipends, 167 pp., 1925.
28. Paschang, Rev. John Linus, J.C.D., The Sacramentals According to the Code of Canon Law, 129 pp., 1925.
29. Piontek, Rev. Cyrillus, O.F.M., S.T.B., J.C.D., De Indulto Exclaustrationis necnon Saecularizationis, XIII-289 pp., 1925.
30. Kearney, Rev. Richard Joseph, S.T.B., J.C.D., Sponsors at Baptism According to the Code of Canon Law, IV-127 pp., 1925.
31. Bartlett, Rev. Chester Joseph, A.M., LL.B., J.C.D., The Tenure of Parochial Property in the United States of America, V-108 pp., 1926.
32. Kilker, Rev. Adrian Jerome, J.C.D., Extreme Unction, V-425 pp., 1926.
33. McCormick, Rev. Robert Emmett, J.C.D., Confessors of Religious, VIII-266 pp., 1926.
34. Miller, Rev. Newton Thomas, J.C.D., Founded Masses According to the Code of Canon Law, VII-93 pp., 1926.
35. Roelker, Rev. Edward G., S.T.D., J.C.D., Principles of Privilege According to the Code of Canon Law, XI-166 pp., 1926.
36. Bakalarczyk, Rev. Richardus, M.I.C., J.U.D., De Novitiatu, VIII-208 pp., 1927.
37. Pizzuti, Rev. Lawrence, O.F.M., J.U.L., De Parochis Religiosis, 1927. (Not Printed.)
38. Bliley, Rev. Nicholas Martin, O.S.B., J.C.D., Altars According to the Code of Canon Law, XIX-132 pp., 1927.
39. Brown, Mr. Brendan Francis, A.B., LL.M., J.U.D., The Canonical Juristic Personality with Special Reference to its Status in the United States of America, V-212 pp., 1927.

40. CAVANAUGH, REV. WILLIAM THOMAS, C.P., J.U.D., The Reservation of the Blessed Sacrament, VIII-101 pp., 1927.
41. DOHENY, REV. WILLIAM J., C.S.C., A.B., J.U.D., Church Property: Modes of Acquisition, X-118 pp., 1927.
42. FELDHAUS, REV. ALOYSIUS H., C.PP.S., J.C.D., Oratories, IX-141 pp., 1927.
43. KELLY, REV. JAMES PATRICK, A.B., J.C.D., The Jurisdiction of the Simple Confessor, X-208 pp., 1927.
44. NEUBERGER, REV. NICHOLAS J., J.C.D., Canon 6 or the Relation of the Codex Juris Canonici to the Preceding Legislation, V-95 pp., 1927.
45. O'KEEFE, REV. GERALD MICHAEL, J.C.D., Matrimonial Dispensations, Powers of Bishops, Priests, and Confessors, VIII-232 pp., 1927.
46. QUIGLEY, REV. JOSEPH A. M., A.B., J.C.D., Condemned Societies, 139 pp., 1927.
47. ZAPLOTNIK, REV. JOHANNES LEO, J.C.D., De Vicariis Foraneis, X-142 pp., 1927.
48. DUSKIE, REV. JOHN ALOYSIUS, A.B., J.C.D., The Canonical Status of the Orientals in the United States, VIII-196 pp., 1928.
49. HYLAND, REV. FRANCIS EDWARD, J.C.D., Excommunication, Its Nature, Historical Development and Effects, VIII-181 pp., 1928.
50. REINMANN, REV. GERALD JOSEPH, O.M.C., J.C.D., The Third Order Secular of Saint Francis, 201 pp., 1928.
51. SCHENK, REV. FRANCIS J., J.C.D., The Matrimonial Impediments of Mixed Religion and Disparity of Cult, XVI-318 pp., 1929.
52. COADY, REV. JOHN JOSEPH, S.T.D., J.U.D., A.M., The Appointment of Pastors, VIII-150 pp., 1929.
53. KAY, REV. THOMAS HENRY, J.C.D., Competence in Matrimonial Procedure, VIII-164 pp., 1929.
54. TURNER, REV. SIDNEY JOSEPH, C.P., J.U.D., The Vow of Poverty, XLIX-217 pp., 1929.
55. KEARNEY, REV. RAYMOND A., A.B., S.T.D., J.C.D., The Principles of Delegation, VII-149 pp., 1929.
56. CONRAN, REV. EDWARD JAMES, A.B., J.C.D., The Interdict, V-163 pp., 1930.
57. O'NEILL, REV. WILLIAM H., J.C.D., Papal Rescripts of Favor, VII-218 pp., 1930.
58. BASTNAGEL, REV. CLEMENT VINCENT, J.U.D., The Appointment of Parochial Adjutants and Assistants, XV-257 pp., 1930.
59. FERRY, REV. WILLIAM A., A.B., J.C.D., Stole Fees, V-136 pp., 1930.
60. COSTELLO, REV. JOHN MICHAEL, A.B., J.C.D., Domicile and Quasi-Domicile, VII-201 pp., 1930.
61. KREMER, REV. MICHAEL NICHOLAS, A.B., S.T.B., J.C.D., Church Support in the United States, VI-136 pp., 1930.
62. ANGULO, REV. LUIS, C.M., J.C.D., Legislation de la Iglesia sobre la intencion en la application de la Santa Misa, VII-104 pp., 1931.

63. Frey, Rev. Wolfgang Norbert, O.S.B., A.B., J.C.D., The Act of Religious Profession, VIII-174 pp., 1931.
64. Roberts, Rev. James Brendan, A.B., J.C.D., The Banns of Marriage, XIV-140 pp., 1931.
65. Ryder, Rev. Raymond Aloysius, A.B., J.C.D., Simony, IX-151 pp., 1931.
66. Campagna, Rev. Angelo, Ph.D., J.U.D., Il Vicario Generale del Vescovo, VII-205 pp., 1931.
67. Cox, Rev. Joseph Godfrey, A.B., J.C.D., The Administration of Seminaries, VI-124 pp., 1931.
68. Gregory, Rev. Donald J., J.U.D., The Pauline Privilege, XV-165 pp., 1931.
69. Donohue, Rev. John F., J.C.D., The Impediment of Crime, VII-110 pp., 1931.
70. Dooley, Rev. Eugene A., O.M.I., J.C.D., Church Law on Sacred Relics, IX-143 pp., 1931.
71. Orth, Rev. Clement Raymond, O.M.C., J.C.D., The Approbation of Religious Institutes, 171 pp., 1931.
72. Pernicone, Rev. Joseph M., A.B., J.C.D., The Ecclesiastical Prohibition of Books, XII-267 pp., 1932.
73. Clinton, Rev. Connell, A.B., J.C.D., The Paschal Precept, IX-108 pp., 1932.
74. Donnelly, Rev. Francis B., A.M., S.T.L., J.C.D., The Diocesan Synod, VIII-125 pp., 1932.
75. Torrente, Rev. Camilo, C.M.F., J.C.D., Las Procesiones Sagradas, V-145 pp., 1932.
76. Murphy, Rev. Edwin J., C.PP.S., J.C.D., Suspension Ex Informata Conscientia, XI-122 pp., 1932.
77. MacKenzie, Rev. Eric F., A.M., S.T.L., J.C.D., The Delict of Heresy in its Commission, Penalization, Absolution, VII-124 pp., 1932.
78. Lyons, Rev. Avitus E., S.T.B., J.C.D., The Collegiate Tribunal of First Instance, XI-147 pp., 1932.
79. Connolly, Rev. Thomas A., J.C.D., Appeals, XI-195 pp., 1932.
80. Sangmeister, Rev. Joseph V., A.B., J.C.D., Force and Fear as Precluding Matrimonial Consent, V-211 pp., 1932.
81. Jaeger, Rev. Leo A., A.B., J.C.D., The Administration of Vacant and Quasi-Vacant Episcopal Sees in the United States, IX-229 pp., 1932.
82. Rimlinger, Rev. Herbert T., J.C.D., Error Invalidating Matrimonial Consent, VII-79 pp., 1932.
83. Barrett, Rev. John D. M., S.S., J.C.D., A Comparative Study of the Third Plenary Council of Baltimore and the Code, IX-221 pp., 1932.
84. Carberry, Rev. John J., Ph.D., S.T.D., J.C.D., The Juridical Form of Marriage, X-177 pp., 1934.
85. Dolan, Rev. John L., A.B., J.C.D., The Defensor Vinculi, XII-157 pp., 1934.

86. Hannan, Rev. Jerome D., A.M., S.T.D., LL.B., J.C.D., The Canon Law of Wills, IX-517 pp., 1934.
87. Lemieux, Rev. Delise A., A.M., J.C.D., The Sentence in Ecclesiastical Procedure, IX-131 pp., 1934.
88. O'Rourke, Rev. James J., A.B., J.C.D., Parish Registers, VII-109 pp., 1934.
89. Timlin, Rev. Bartholomew, O.F.M., A.M., J.C.D., Conditional Matrimonial Consent, X-381 pp., 1934.
90. Wahl, Rev. Francis X., A.B., J.C.D., The Matrimonial Impediments of Consanguinity and Affinity, VI-125 pp., 1934.
91. White, Rev. Robert J., A.B., LL.B., S.T.B., J.C.D., Canonical Ante-Nuptial Promises and the Civil Law, VI-152 pp., 1934.
92. Herrera, Rev. Antonio Parra, O.C.D., J.C.D., Legislacion Ecclesiastica sobra el Ayuno y la Abstinencia, XI-191 pp., 1935.
93. Kennedy, Rev. Edwin J., J.C.D., The Special Matrimonial Process in Cases of Evident Nullity, X-165 pp., 1935.
94. Manning, Rev. John J., A.B., J.C.D., Presumption of Law in Matrimonial Procedure, XI-111 pp., 1935.
95. Moeder, Rev. John M., J.C.D., The Proper Bishop for Ordination and Dimissorial Letters, VII-135 pp., 1935.
96. O'Mara, Rev. William A., A.B., J.C.D., Canonical Causes for Matrimonial Dispensations, IX-155 pp., 1935.
97. Reilly, Rev. Peter, J.C.D., Residence of Pastors, IX-81 pp., 1935.
98. Smith, Rev. Mariner T., O.P., S.T.Lr., J.C.D., The Penal Law for Religious, VII-169 pp., 1935.
99. Whalen, Rev. Donald W., A.M., J.C.D., The Value of Testimonial Evidence in Matrimonial Procedure, XIII-297 pp., 1935.
100. Cleary, Rev. Joseph F., J.C.D., Canonical Limitations on the Alienation of Church Property, VIII-141 pp., 1936.
101. Glynn, Rev. John C., J.C.D., The Promoter of Justice, XX-337 pp., 1936.
102. Brennan, Rev. James H., S.S., M.A., S.T.B., J.C.D., The Simple Convalidation of Marriage, VI-135 pp., 1937.
103. Brunini, Rev. Joseph Bernard, J.C.D., The Clerical Obligations of Canons 139 and 142, X-121 pp., 1937.
104. Connor, Rev. Maurice, A.B., J.C.D., The Administrative Removal of Pastors, VIII-159 pp., 1937.
105. Guilfoyle, Rev. Merlin Joseph, J.C.D., Custom, XI-144 pp., 1937.
106. Hughes, Rev. James Austin, A.B., A.M., J.C.D., Witnesses in Criminal Trials of Clerics, IX-140 pp., 1937.
107. Jansen, Rev. Raymond J., A.B., S.T.L., J.C.D., Canonical Provisions for Catechetical Instruction, VII-153 pp., 1937.
108. Kealy, Rev. John James, A.B., J.C.D., The Introductory Libellus in Church Court Procedure, XI-121 pp., 1937.

109. McManus, Rev. James Edward, C.SS.R., J.C.D., The Administration of Temporal Goods in Religious Institutes, XVI-196 pp., 1937.
110. Moriarty, Rev. Eugene James, J.C.D., Oaths in Ecclesiastical Courts, X-115 pp., 1937.
111. Rainer, Rev. Eligius George, C.SS.R., J.C.D., Suspension of Clerics, XVII-249 pp., 1937.
112. Reilly, Rev. Thomas F., C.SS.R., J.C.D., Visitation of Religious, VI-195 pp., 1938.
113. Moriarity, Rev. Francis E., C.SS.R., J.C.D., The Extraordinary Absolution from Censures, XV-334 pp., 1938.
114. Connolly, Rev. Nicholas P., J.C.D., The Canonical Erection of Parishes, X-132 pp., 1938.
115. Donovan, Rev. James Joseph, J.C.D., The Pastor's Obligation in Prenuptial Investigation, XII-322 pp., 1938.
116. Harrigan, Rev. Robert J., M.A., S.T.B., J.C.D., The Radical Sanation of Invalid Marriages, VIII-208 pp., 1938.
117. Boffa, Rev. Conrad Humbert, J.C.D., Canonical Provisions for Catholic Schools, VII-211 pp., 1939.
118. Parsons, Rev. Anscar John, O.M.Cap., J.C.D., Canonical Elections, XII-236 pp., 1939.
119. Reilly, Rev. Edward Michael, A.B., J.C.D., The General Norms of Dispensation, XII-156 pp., 1939.
120. Ryan, Rev. Gerald Aloysius, A.B., J.C.D., Principles of Episcopal Jurisdiction, XII-172 pp., 1939.
121. Burton, Rev. Francis James, C.S.C., A.B., J.C.D., A Commentary on Canon 1125, X-222 pp., 1940.
122. Miaskiewicz, Rev. Francis Sigismund, J.C.D., Supplied Jurisdiction According to Canon 209, XII-340 pp., 1940.
123. Rice, Rev. Patrick William, A.B., J.C.D., Proof of Death in Prenuptial Investigation, VIII-156 pp., 1940.
124. Anglin, Rev. Thomas Francis, M.S., J.C.D., The Eucharistic Fast, VIII-183 pp., 1941.
125. Coleman, Rev. John Jerome, J.C.D., The Minister of Confirmation, VI-153 pp., 1941.
126. Downs, Rev. John Emmanuel, A.B., J.C.D., The Concept of Clerical Immunity, XI-163 pp., 1941.
127. Esswein, Rev. Anthony Albert, J.C.D., Extrajudicial Penal Powers of Ecclesiastical Superiors, X-144 pp., 1941.
128. Farrell, Rev. Benjamin Francis, M.A., S.T.L., J.C.D., The Rights and Duties of the Local Ordinary Regarding Congregations of Women Religious of Pontifical Approval, V-195 pp., 1941.
129. Feeney, Rev. Thomas John, A.B., S.T.L., J.C.D., Restitutio in Integrum, VI-169 pp., 1941.
130. Findlay, Rev. Stephen William, O.S.B., A.B., J.C.D., Canonical

Norms Governing the Deposition and Degradation of Clerics, XVII-279 pp., 1941.

131. Goodwine, Rev. John, A.B., S.T.L., J.C.D., The Right of the Church to Acquire Property, VIII-119 pp., 1941.
132. Heston, Rev. Edward Louis, C.S.C., Ph.D., S.T.D., J.C.D., The Alienation of Church Property in the United States, XII-222 pp., 1941.
133. Hogan, Rev. James John, A.B., S.T.L., J.C.D., Judicial Advocates and Procurators, XIII-200 pp., 1941.
134. Kealy, Rev. Thomas M., A.B., Litt.B., J.C.D., Dowry of Women Religious, IX-152 pp., 1941.
135. Keene, Rev. Michael James, O.S.B., J.C.D., Religious Ordinaries and Canon 198, V-164 pp., 1942.
136. Kerin, Rev. Charles A., S.S., M.A., S.T.B., J.C.D., The Privation of Christian Burial, XVI-279 pp., 1941.
137. Louis, Rev. William Francis, M.A., J.C.D., Diocesan Archives, X-101 pp., 1941.
138. McDevitt, Rev. Gilbert Joseph, A.B., J.C.D., Legitimacy and Legitimation, X-247 pp., 1941.
139. McDonough, Rev. Thomas Joseph, A.B., J.C.D., Apostolic Administrators, X-217 pp., 1941.
140. **Meier, Rev. Carl Anthony, A.B., J.C.D., Penal Administrative Pro**cedure Against Negligent Pastors, XI-240 pp., 1941.
141. Schmidt, Rev. John Rogg, A.B., J.C.D., The Principles of Authentic Interpretation in Canon 17 of the Code of Canon Law, XII-331 pp., 1941.
142. Slafkosky, Rev. Andrew Leonard, A.B., J.C.D., The Canonical Episcopal Visitation of the Diocese, X-197 pp., 1941.
143. Swoboda, Rev. Innocent Robert, O.F.M., J.C.D., Ignorance in Relation to the Imputability of Delicts, IX-271 pp., 1941.
144. Dubé, Rev. Arthur Joseph, A.B., J.C.D., The General Principles for the Reckoning of Time in Canon Law, VIII-299 pp., 1941.
145. McBride, Rev. James T., A.B., J.C.D., Incardination and Excardination of Seculars, XX-585 pp., 1941.
146 Król, Rev. John T., J.C.D., The Defendant in Ecclesiastical Trials, XII-207 pp., 1942.
147. Comyns, Rev. Joseph J., C.SS.R., A.B., J.C.D., Papal and Episcopal Administration of Church Property, XIV-155 pp., 1942.
148. Barry, Rev. Garrett Francis, O.M.I., J.C.D., Violation of the Cloister, XII-260 pp., 1942.
149. Bolduc, Rev. Gatien, C.S.V., A.B., S.T.L., J.C.D., Les Études dans les Religions Cléricales, VIII-155 pp., 1942.
150. Boyle, Rev. David John, M.A., J.C.D., The Juridic Effects of Moral Certitude on Pre-Nuptial Guarantees, XII-188 pp., 1942.
151. **Canavan, Rev. Walter Joseph, M.A., Litt.D., J.C.D., The Profes**sion of Faith, XII-143 pp., 1942.

152. Desrochers, Rev. Bruno, A.B., Ph.L., S.T.B., J.C.D., Le Premier Concile Plénier de Québéc et le Code de Droit Canonique, XIV–186 pp., 1942.
153. Dillon, Rev. Robert Edward, A.B., J.C.D., Common Law Marriage, X-148 pp., 1942.
154. Dodwell, Rev. Edward John, Ph.D., S.T.B., J.C.D., The Time and Place for the Celebration of Marriage, X-156 pp., 1942.
155. Donnellan, Rev. Thomas Andrew, A.B., J.C.D., The Obligation of the Missa pro Populo, VII-131 pp., 1942.
156. Eltz, Rev. Louis Anthony, A.B., J.C.D., Cooperation in Crime, XII-208 pp., 1942.
157. Gass, Rev. Sylvester Francis, M.A., J.C.D., Ecclesiastical Pensions, XI-206 pp., 1942.
158. Guiniven, Rev. John Joseph, C.SS.R., J.C.D., The Precept of Hearing Mass, XIV-188 pp., 1942.
159. Gluczynski, Rev. John Theophilus, J.C.D., The Desecration and Violation of Churches, X-126 pp., 1942.
160. Hammill, Rev. John Leo, M.A., J.C.D., The Obligations of the Traveler According to Canon 14, VIII-204 pp., 1942.
161. Haydt, Rev. John Joseph, A.B., J.C.D., Reserved Benefices, XI-148 pp., 1942.
162. Huser, Rev. Roger John, O.F.M., A.B., J.C.D., The Crime of Abortion in Canon Law, XII-187 pp., 1942.
163. Kearney, Rev. Francis Patrick, A.B., S.T.L., J.C.D., The Principles of Canon 1127, X-162 pp., 1942.
164. Linahen, Rev. Leo James, S.T.L., J.C.D., De Absolutione Complicis In Peccato Turpi, 114 pp., 1942.
165. McCloskey, Rev. Joseph Aloysius, A.B., J.C.D., The Subject of Ecclesiastical Law According to Canon 12, XVII-246 pp., 1942.
166. O'Neill, Rev. Francis Joseph, C.SS.R., J.C.D., The Dismissal of Religious in Temporary Vows, XIII-220 pp., 1942.
167. Prince, Rev. John Edward, A.B., S.T.B., J.C.D., The Diocesan Chancellor, X-136 pp., 1942.
168. Riesner, Rev. Albert Joseph, C.SS.R., J.C.D., Apostates and Fugitives from Religious Institutes, IX-168 pp., 1942.
169. Stenger, Rev. Joseph Bernard, J.C.D., The Mortgaging of Church Property, 186 pp., 1942.
170. Waldron, Rev. Joseph Francis, A.B., J.C.D., The Minister of Baptism, XII-197 pp., 1942.
171. Willett, Rev. Robert Albert, J.C.D., The Probative Value of Documents in Ecclesiastical Trials, X-124 pp., 1942.
172. Woeber, Rev. Edward Martin, M.A., J.C.D., The Interpellations, XII-161 pp., 1942.
173. Benko, Rev. Matthew Aloysius, O.S.B., M.A., J.C.D., The Abbot *Nullius*, XVI-148 pp., 1943.

174. CHRIST, REV. JOSEPH JAMES, M.A., S.T.L., J.C.D., Dispensation from Vindicative Penalties, XIV-285 pp., 1943.
175. CLANCY, REV. PATRICK M. J., O.P., A.B., S.T.Lr., J.C.D., The Local Religious Superior, X-229 pp., 1943.
176. CLARKE, REV. THOMAS JAMES, J.C.D., Parish Societies, XII-147 pp., 1943.
177. CONNOLLY, REV. JOHN PATRICK, S.T.L., J.C.D., Synodal Examiners and Parish Priest Consultors, X-223 pp., 1943.
178. DRUMM, REV. WILLIAM MARTIN, A.B., J.C.D., Hospital Chaplains, XII-175 pp., 1943.
179. FLANAGAN, REV. BERNARD JOSEPH, A.B., S.T.L., J.C.D., The Canonical Erection of Religious Houses, X-147 pp., 1943.
180. KELLEHER, REV. STEPHEN JOSEPH, A.B., S.T.B., J.C.D., Discussions with Non-Catholics: Canonical Legislation, X-93 pp., 1943.
181. LEWIS, REV. GORDIAN, C.P., J.C.D., Chapters in Religious Institutes, XII-169 pp., 1943.
182. MARX, REV. ADOLPH, J.C.D., The Declaration of Nullity of Marriages Contracted Outside the Church, X-151 pp., 1943.
183. MATULENAS, REV. RAYMOND ANTHONY, O.S.B., A.B., J.C.D., Communication, a Source of Privileges, XII-225 pp., 1943.
184. O'LEARY, REV. CHARLES GERARD, C.SS.R., J.C.D., Religious Dismissed After Perpetual Profession, X-213 pp., 1943.
185. POWER, REV. CORNELIUS MICHAEL, J.C.D., The Blessing of Cemeteries, XII-231 pp., 1943.
186. SHUHLER, REV. RALPH VINCENT, O.S.A., J.C.D., Privileges of Regulars to Absolve and Dispense, XII-195 pp., 1943.
187. ZIOLKOWSKI, REV. THADDEUS STANISLAUS, A.B., J.C.D., The Consecration and Blessing of Churches, XII-151 pp., 1943.
188. HENEGHAN, REV. JOHN JOSEPH, S.T.D., J.C.D., The Marriages of Unworthy Catholics: Canons 1065 and 1066, XVI-213 pp., 1944.
189. CARROLL, REV. COLEMAN FRANCIS, M.A., S.T.L., J.C.L., Charitable Institutions.
190. CIESLUK, REV. JOSEPH EDWARD, Ph.B., S.T.L., J.C.D., National Parishes in the United States, VI-178 pp., 1944.
191. COBURN, REV. VINCENT PAUL, A.B., J.C.D., Marriages of Conscience, XII-172 pp., 1944.
192. CONNORS, REV. CHARLES PAUL, C.S.Sp., A.B., J.C.D., Extra-Judicial Procurators in the Code of Canon Law, X-94 pp., 1944.
193. COYLE, REV. PAUL RAYMOND, A.B., J.C.D., Judicial Exceptions, X-142 pp., 1944.
194. FAIR, REV. BARTHOLOMEW FRANCIS, A.B., S.T.L., J.C.D., The Impediment of Abduction, XII-122 pp., 1944.
195. GALLAGHER, REV. THOMAS RAPHAEL, O.P., A.B., S.T.Lr., J.C.D., The Examination of the Qualities of the Ordinand, X-166 pp., 1944.
196. GANNON, REV. JOHN MARK, S.T.L., J.C.D., The Interstices Required for the Promotion to Orders, XII-100 pp., 1944.

**197. Goldsmith, Rev. J. William, B.C.S., S.T.L., J.C.D., The Competence of Church and State over Marriage—Disputed Points, X-128 pp., 1944.**

198. Goodwine, Rev. Joseph Gerard, A.B., S.T.D., J.C.D., The Reception of Converts, XIV-326 pp., 1944.

199. Kowalski, Rev. Romuald Eugene, O.F.M., A.B., J.C.D., Sustenance of Religious Houses of Regulars, X-174 pp., 1944.

200. McCoy, Rev. Alan Edward, O.F.M., J.C.D., Force and Fear in Relation to Delictual Imputability and Penal Responsibility, XII-160 pp., 1944.

201. McDevitt, Rev. Vincent John, Ph.B., S.T.L., J.C.L., Perjury.

202. Martin, Rev. Thomas Owen, Ph.D., S.T.D., J.C.D., Adverse Possession, Prescription and Limitation of Actions: The Canonical "Praescriptio," XX-208 pp., 1944.

203. Miklosovic, Rev. Paul John, A.B., J.C.L., Attempted Marriages and Their Consequent Juridic Effects.

**204. Mundy, Rev. Thomas Maurice, A.B., S.T.L., J.C.D., The Union of Parishes, X—164 pp., 1944.**

205. O'Dea, Rev. John Coyle, A.B., J.C.D., The Matrimonial Impediment of Nonage, VIII-126 pp., 1944.

206. Olalia, Rev. Alexander Ayson, S.T.L., J.C.D., A Comparative Study of the Christian Constitution of States and the Constitution of the Philippine Commonwealth, XII—136 pp., 1944.

207. Poisson, Rev. Pierre-Marie, C.S.C., A.B., Ph.L., Th.L., J.C.L., Droits Patrimoniaux des Maisons et des Églises Religieuses.

208. Stadalnikas, Rev. Casimir Joseph, M.I.C., J.C.D., Reservation of Censures, X-141 pp., 1944.

**209. Sullivan, Rev. Eugene Henry, S.T.L., J.C.D., Proof of the Reception of the Sacraments, X—165 pp., 1944.**

210. Vaughan, Rev. William Edward, J.C.D., Constitutions for Diocesan Courts, X-210 pp., 1944.

**211. Paro, Rev. Gino, S.T.D., J.C.L., The Right of Apostolic Legation.**

212. Balzer, Rev. Ralph Francis, C.P., J.C.D., The Computation of Time in a Canonical Novitiate, X—227 pp., 1945.

213. Dougherty, Rev. John Whelan, A.B., S.T.L., J.C.D., De Inquisitione Speciali, XII—195 pp., 1945.

214. Dziob, Rev. Michael Walter, J.C.D., The Sacred Congregation for the Oriental Church, XII—181 pp., 1945.

215. Eidenschink, Rev. John Albert, O.S.B., B.A., J.C.D, The Election of Bishops in the Letters of Pope Gregory the Great, VII—200 pp., 1945.

216. Gill, Rev. Nicholas, C.P., J.C.D., The Spiritual Prefect in Clerical Religious Houses of Study, X—140 pp., 1945.

**217. Hynes, Rev. Harry Gerard, S.T.L., J.C.D., The Privileges of Cardinals, XII-183 pp., 1945.**

**218. McDevitt, Rev. Gerald Vincent, S.T.L., J.C.D., The Renunciation** of an Ecclesiastical Office, XIV—179 pp., 1945.

219. Manning, Rev. Joseph Leroy, J.C.D., The Free Conferral of Offices, VIII—116 pp., 1945.
220. **Meyer, Rev. Louis G., O.S.B., A.B., S.T.B., J.C.D., Alms-Gathering** by Religious, XII—163 pp., 1945.
221. O'Donnell, Rev. Cletus Francis, M.A., J.C.D., The Marriage of Minors, XII—268 pp., 1945.
222. **Prunskis, Rev. Joseph, J.C.D., Comparative Law, Ecclesiastical and Civil, in Lithuanian Concordat, X—161 pp., 1945.**
223. **Sweeney, Rev. Francis Patrick, C.SS.R., J.C.D., The Reduction of Clerics to the Lay State, X—199 pp., 1945.**
224. Vogelpohl, Rev. Henry John, J.C.D., The Simple Impediments to Holy Orders, XVI—190 pp., 1945.
225. Brockhaus, Rev. Thomas Aquinas, O.S.B., A.B., J.C.D., Religious who Are Known as *Conversi*, X—127 pp., 1945.
226. Griese, Rev. N. Orville, S.T.D., J.C.D., The Marriage Contract and the Procreation of Offspring, XVI-224 pp., 1946.
227. Boudreaux, Rev. Warren Louis, J.C.D., The "*ab acatholicis nati*" of Canon 1099, § 2, XII-110 pp., 1946.
228. Bowe, Rev. Thomas Joseph, A.B., J.C.D., Religious Superioresses, VIII-206 pp., 1946.
229. Diederichs, Rev. Michael Ferdinand, S.C.J., J.C.D., The Jurisdiction of the Latin Ordinaries over their Oriental Subjects, XIV-153 pp., 1946.
230. Dingman, Rev. Maurice John, A.B., S.T.L., J.C.L., The Plaintiff in Contentious Trials.
231. Frison, Rev. Basil, C.M.F., M.Mus., J.C.D., The Retroactivity of Law, X-221 pp., 1946.
232. Galvin, Rev. William Anthony, M.A., J.C.D., The Administrative Transfer of Pastors, XII-288 pp., 1946.
233. Goracy, Rev. Joseph C., J.C.L., The Diriment Matrimonial Impediment of Major Orders.
234. Hale, Rev. Joseph Francis, M.A., S.T.L., J.C.L., The Pastor of Burial.
235. Henry, Rev. Joseph Arthur, A.B., J.C.D., The Mass and Holy Communion: Inter-Ritual Law, XII-138 pp., 1946.
236. Linenberger, Rev. Herbert, C.PP.S., J.C.L., The False Denunciation of an Innocent Confessor.
237. Lowry, Rev. James Martin, A.B., J.C.D., Dispensation from Private Vows, XII-266 pp., 1946.
238. Lynch, Rev. George Edward, A.B., S.T.L., J.C.D., Coadjutors and Auxiliaries of Bishops, X-107 pp., 1947.
239. Lynch, Rev. Timothy, M.S.SS.T., J.C.D., Contracts between Bishops and Religious Congregations, XIV-232 pp., 1946.
240. McClunn, Rev. Justin David, A.B., S.T.L., J.C.D., Administrative Recourse, VII-142 pp., 1946.

241. Lohmuller, Rev. Martin Nicholas, A.B., J.C.D., The Promulgation of Law, XII-140 pp., 1947.
242. McGrath, Rev. James, A.B., J.C.D., The Privilege of the Canon, XII-156 pp., 1946.
243. Marbach, Rev. Joseph Francis, A.B., J.C.D., Marriage Legislation for the Catholics of the Oriental Rites in the United States and Canada, XIV-314 pp., 1946.
244. Shimkus, Rev. Bernard Aloysius, A.B., J.C.L., The Determination and Transfer of Rite.
245. Smith, Rev. Vincent Michael, A.B., S.T.L., J.C.L., Ignorance Affecting Matrimonial Consent.
246. Wachtrle, Rev. Paul Anthony, A.B., J.C.L., The Baptism of the Children of Non-Catholics.
247. Crotty, Rev. Matthew Michael, J.C.D., The Recipient of First Holy Communion, X-142 pp., 1947.
248. Eagleton, Rev. George, J.C.L., The Quinquennial Faculties, Formula IV.
249. Gibbons, Rev. Marion Leo, C.M., J.C.D., Domicile of the Wife Unlawfully Separated from Her Husband, XIV-171 pp., 1947.
250. Kelly, Rev. Bernard Matthew, S.T.L., J.C.D., The Functions Reserved to Pastors, X-150 pp., 1947.
251. Kilcullen, Rev. Thomas John, LL.M., J.C.D., The Collegiate Moral Person as Party Litigant, X-150 pp., 1947.
252. Lafontaine, Rev. Germain Joseph, W.F., J.C.L., Relations Canoniques entre le Missionaire et Ses Superieurs.
253. Lane, Rev. Loras Thomas, J.C.L., Matrimonial Procedure in Ordinary Court of Second Instance.
254. Lover, Rev. James Francis, C.Ss.R., J.C.D., The Master of Novices, X-168 pp., 1947.
255. McNicholas, Rev. Timothy Joseph, J.C.L., The *Septimae Manus* Witness.
256. Marositz, Rev. Joseph John, M.S.C., J.C.D., Obligations and Privileges of Religious Promoted to the Episcopal or Cardinalitial Dignities, XII-180 pp. 1947.
257. Murphy, Rev. Francis Joseph, J.C.D., Legislative Powers of the Provincial Council, XII-158 pp., 1947.
258. O'Brien, Rev. Romaeus William, O.Carm., J.C.D., The Provincial Superior in Religious Orders of Men, X-294 pp., 1947.
259. Pfaller, Rev. Benedict Anthony, O.S.B., J.C.L., *The ipso facto* Effected Dismissal of Religious.
260. Popek, Rev. Alphonse Sylvester, J.C.D., The Rights and Obligations of Metropolitans, XVIII-460 pp., 1947.
261. Ristuccia, Rev. Bernard Joseph, C.M., J.C.L., Quasi-Religious.
262. Sonntag, Rev. Nathaniel Louis, O.F.M.Cap., J.C.D., Censorship of Special Classes of Books, XII-147 pp., 1947.

263. STADLER, REV. JOSEPH NICHOLAS, J.C.L., Frequent Holy Communion.
264. SZAL, REV. IGNATIUS JOSEPH, J.C.L., The Communication of Catholics with Schismatics, XII-217 pp., 1947.
265. WAGNER, REV. URBAN STANLEY, O.F.M.Conv., J.C.D., Parochial Substitute Vicars and Supplying Priests, IX-126 pp., 1947.

www.ingramcontent.com/pod-product-compliance
Lightning Source LLC
LaVergne TN
LVHW050210080826
844660LV00012B/390

* 9 7 8 0 8 1 3 2 2 4 3 3 6 *